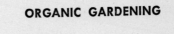

ORGANIC GARDENING

Books by J. I. Rodale

ORGANIC GARDENING
PAY DIRT
THE HEALTHY HUNZAS
THE HEALTH FINDER
THE WORD FINDER
THE PHRASE FINDER

by J. I. RODALE

ORGANIC GARDENING:

HOW TO GROW

HEALTHY VEGETABLES

FRUITS AND FLOWERS

USING NATURE'S OWN METHODS

 HANOVER HOUSE, GARDEN CITY, NEW YORK

CONTENTS

ORGANIC GARDENING

WHAT IS ORGANIC GARDENING?

Very briefly, organic gardening or farming is a system whereby a fertile soil is maintained by applying Nature's own law of replenishing it—that is, the addition and preservation of humus, the use of organic matter instead of chemical fertilizers, and, of course, the making of a compost pile and mulching. Organiculture is a vigorous and growing movement, one that is destined to alter our concepts of the garden and the farm and to revolutionize our methods of operating them in order to secure for ourselves more abundant and more perfect food. The seed sown by Sir Albert Howard, the great pioneer in organic farming, is beginning to bloom lustily and with such vim that it is already thriving and propagating by its own strength. Composters by the thousands are telling their neighbors of the wonders of this new, yet in reality age-old, method, and they in turn are listening and beginning to follow. Compost heaps are becoming an integral part of the farm, the garden, and the landscape. Organiculture is here to stay. When it is possible to see astounding results obtained by one's own hand, a quick good-by is said to groping and artificial test-tube methods.

It may be advisable at this point to list the basic precepts of the organic method and to outline organic practices for the benefit of newcomers, for the approval of seasoned veterans, and for the possible conversion of scoffers and skeptics, some of whom attack it without knowing exactly what they are futilely endeavoring to combat.

What the Organic Gardener Believes and Practices

Human health is more precious than quick profits and insect-free crops. Any methods to bolster yields should be adopted only after we are thoroughly convinced that future generations will not be injured. Increased yields will come with the intense practice of the organic methods and the proper lapse of time.

The balance of Nature must be respected. Each part has its own sphere of activity as well as fusing with and complementing other related parts. A substance that alters one part, for instance, may affect half a dozen others—most often to our own disadvantage. Spraying, for example, kills off beneficial insects and birds, contaminates the soil, leaves poisonous residues on crops, and is a financial burden on the farmer.

The soil is a storehouse of living organisms which must be fed and cared for as any others. Bacteria, fungi, insects, and earthworms inhabit it by the millions, using organic matter as food and in turn preparing it for living plants. Concentrated chemicals, on the other hand, cannot be continually added to the soil to destroy harmful insects and disease organisms without harming the needed beneficial micro-organisms.

Plants fed with natural fertilizers are well balanced in trace elements and vitamins. The use of chemical fertilizers, such as superphosphate, may supply an excess of phosphorus while crowding out magnesium. Well-nourished plants are more resistant to insect attack than deficient crops, probably through odor and vitamin abnormalities. These two theories were recently supported by experiments at the Bartlett Tree Expert Company and at the University of California.

The organic gardener, of course, realizes that fertilization is not the only measure for success. He must treat the soil as a living, breathing entity. Compost alone does not make a successful gardener any more than does gardening without compost. The organic farmer observes the law of return, restoring to the soil all plant residues that come from it. He does not burn leaves, spoiled hay, or other crop by-products, but often goes out of his way to retrieve organic matter that others throw away. He is against the operation of hundred-thousand-acre farm factories where all the basic principles of organic farming are violated or ignored. The organiculturist believes also that infertile soils should be set aside for the growing of chemurgic crops only—for example, non-food crops such as tobacco, cotton for clothes, and similar types of plant commodities.

Chemical Fertilizers

Many fertilizers now on the market have been tested only briefly. We condemn these chemical fertilizers because they contain certain poisonous elements in too great a concentration. While it is true that all the chemicals present in these artificial fertilizers are also distributed in ocean waters, the quantities are so exceedingly negligible that fish can safely swim in such a medium. No concentrated, completely soluble fertilizers are recommended in the organic method. Recent controlled experiments with aphids in the United States Government Agricultural Stations showed that the more chemical fertilizers were used, the more attractive the plants became to the aphids.

Relying on harsh chemicals year after year will produce nutritionally poor crops. Flooding plant roots with these chemical fertilizers may cause trace-element deficiencies. The soil becomes strongly acid, unless lime is constantly applied. Earthworms and beneficial bacteria and fungi are driven away or killed. Toxic residues, such as chlorides and sulfates, build up year after year. Lastly, organic matter is quickly depleted from chemically fertilized soils.

Fertilizing the Soil the Natural or Organic Way

The organic gardener believes that only suitable organic matter should go back to the land, either by mulching or composting. A mulch is a layer of organic matter (plant or animal wastes), placed on the soil surface, which protects the land while fertilizing it. Only those materials which ordinarily are not applied directly to the soil (garbage, for example) need be composted. Organic matter can be piled in bins, pits, or open heaps to decay, or compost. This method, however, often reduces the mineral content of fresh organic matter, and mulching is therefore frequently preferred.

Besides compost made of plant matter, the organiculturist usually employs as fertilizers such substances as raw phosphate rock, dolomite, ground oyster shells, and miscellaneous ground rocks such as granite dusts and pulverized limestone. Quicklime, on the other hand, is much too strong in action and will destroy bacteria. Wood ashes may be used as a substitute for lime in making compost.

Raw ground phosphate rock and colloidal phosphate supply phosphorus, while glauconite marl and granite dust release potash. These fertilizers dissolve slowly, benefiting crops for several years. Rock fertilizers, in addition, do not leach quickly into the drainage waters. Millions of tons of natural rock fertilizers await further discovery by enlightened fertilizer companies. The supply of such rock materials is enormous and cheap, and recent experimental work has already demonstrated that, if ground fine enough, they become a quick-acting fertilizer. Many rocks contain plant nutrients in considerable amounts which are insoluble until they are pulverized and brought into contact with the soil, where they are rendered soluble by carbonic acid and other mild acids in the soil. Meanwhile, however, better results can be obtained if the chemicals we use are in organic form.

Another tenet of the organiculturists is the making of compost by Sir Albert Howard's Indore process, involving the ratio of one part animal matter to three parts of plant residue, a relationship which is found naturally in field and forest. Many persons mistakenly consider themselves practicers of organiculture if they simply use manure, which is in itself an unbalanced fertilizer. Manure does, to be sure, contain many valuable elements, including vitamins and hormones; but inasmuch as plants, and especially leaves, are extremely rich in mineral elements, we ought to use both plant and animal matter. Where manure alone is used, it must be well rotted. The same applies to green matter, which should be rotted through the compost heap. The plowing under of raw green matter or raw manure before the proper soil micro-organisms can bring about their decay is a severe shock to the soil. Eventually such organic matter will benefit the soil, but in the meantime the current crop will suffer because of a sort of indigestion. In mulching, however, the raw matter remains on the surface and therefore does not involve the activities of the soil micro-organisms which can work in the interests of the growing crop.

Sprays and Dusts

The use of poison sprays in orchards and on farm crops is taboo, for there is definite evidence to confirm the fact that the strengthening of a plant or tree by the use of compost makes the plant or tree much less susceptible to infestation by insects or disease than does recourse to sprays. The organiculturist believes that even on a commercial scale orcharding can eventually eliminate dependence on poison sprays.

It is interesting to note that a prominent scientist recently remarked that sprays and dusts which destroy insects certainly are not free from some toxicity for human beings. The same can be said about potent weed killers, fungicides, and other chemicals that violently disturb the natural functions of plant and animal life. The highly popular hormone sprays, for example, were given hasty official acceptance without thorough study of the side effects on fruits and vegetables. It is well to keep these facts in mind when tempted to invest in spray equipment. The least toxic of insecticides are plant extracts such as rotenone or derris dust, which should be applied only when absolutely necessary. A conscientious organic gardener, however, will try to avoid using them.

Safe Control of Insects and Pests

It is true that some natural insect controls may be necessary until, and possibly after, the gardener has been practicing the organic method for several years. The soil must become rich and fertile; insect parasites and predators must be encouraged. Safe measures for control are hand-picking of insect pests, encouraging birds, interplanting with crops that repel insects, planting resistant varieties, and setting out traps and attractant lamps. Exterminating all harmful insects is not our goal; good yields, truly safe food, and sensible insect controls is the answer.

"Chemical" and "Organic"

Sometimes a chemist takes us to task and criticizes the inclusion of certain items in the organic arsenal of weapons. For example, he calls lime a chemical, yet we advocate its presence in the compost heap. Of course lime is a chemical. So is everything else. There is nitrogen, phosphorus, and potash in your tablecloth, in ham and eggs, and in your very own mother-in-law! So it is high time that we and our adversaries stop talking in elusive generalities and start to clarify our specific points.

In regard to the word "organic," Webster says, "Pertaining to, or derived from, living organisms." On the other hand—also according to Webster—when a chemist refers to the word "organic" he means "Pertaining to or designating that branch of chemistry which treats of the carbon compounds produced in plants and animals. . . ." It can be seen, therefore, that when we say "organic" we mean something different from what the chemist understands by that word, but these are mere technicalities resulting from professionalized word usage. We do not exclude a chemical simply because it is a chemical any more than we include an organism just because it is an organism. There are, however, some chemicals and some bacteria that try to upset everything that the organiculturist is attempting to achieve. *Those* saboteurs are the ones against which we discriminate.

TWO

THE SOIL

Soil is the more or less loose layer of the earth's surface, as distinguished from the solid rock that is usually beneath it. Originally there was a time when there was no soil, when the earth was one mass of rock and there were no plants of any kind. The rock was the parent, the precursor of the soil as we know it today. Through the action of certain agencies, part of this rock was transformed into soil. For millions of years this rock has been "weathering"—that is, decomposing by the action of hot and cold air, winds, rains, fogs, the movement of glaciers, and by climatic changes. Professor Albrecht of the University of Missouri recently said, "What is soil after all? It is a temporary rest-stop while the rock is on its way to the sea." In other words, the rock gradually forms into soil, which is washed by erosion into the bottom of the seas where, over a period of millions of years, it will harden again into rock.

Rocks

Rocks are porous—more so than can be noticed with the naked eye. They absorb water, and exposure to varying temperatures causes a crumbling and a breaking. Running water and the action of glaciers moving over the rocks soften and grind them. These continuing actions keep pulverizing, breaking down, and disintegrating them into finer and finer powdery masses. The action of the carbonic-acid gas which enters the water from the air also helps, with its acidic solvent action, to soften the rock.

Practically none of these rocks contain nitrogen, which is so prevalent in the air and in the soil. However, in order for plants to grow, they must have some of this element. The rocks contain all the *minerals* needed for plant growth, but nitrogen had to come from the air at the beginning of the process of formation of soil. The air, containing 78 per cent nitrogen, had more than enough for that purpose.

First Plant Life

The evolution of plant life was an elaborate, long-time process, taking millions of years in time. The first plants that were able to grow were extremely simple ones, such as the lichens and the mosses that appeared on the face of the rocks. Their requirements for sustenance were not too great. Certain bacteria which had already come into existence took a prominent part in helping them to grow—feeding upon the minerals that were in the rock and upon the nitrogen in the air. It is certain that bacteria came before the lichens and mosses died. The remains of the lichens and mosses were the first sources of organic matter and, mixed with the minuscule rock fragments, became our first soils. Thus the soil was a mixture of rock particles and organic matter.

During the process of decay of the lichens and the mosses, certain substances were given off, such as carbonic acid and other humus types of acid, which worked upon the rock to make more mineral food available for the future plants. The action of air and carbonic acid on the rock particles and on the organic matter turned the substances dark, which is a characteristic in the formation of humus. Soon there was sufficient soil so that plants higher up in the scale of plant life could live, and by that inexorable process of slow evolution in living matter, ferns came into existence and were able to grow. During millions of years of slow evolution, still higher plants began to evolve, such as grasses and shrubs. Finally, trees began to grow.

The soil consisted primarily of weathered rock fragments, water, organic matter, and dusts which fell upon it from the air. Lightning charged nitrogen into the soil; rains washed nitrogen and other elements into it. Soil bacteria extracted nitrogen from the air. But basically you can visualize the soil as being made up mainly of weathered rock particles and organic matter, closely associated and mixed together.

How to Feed the Soil

In the organic method of gardening, we attempt to feed the soil in such a manner that its natural constitution is not disturbed, basing our procedures and techniques on the study of the make-up of the soil. Now that we know how it was originally formed, we can better understand what kind of food will suit it.

We have learned that the soil is made up of inorganic minerals formed from rock fragments. It also contains organic matter, water, and air. Those are its four basic elements. Therefore it is not unreasonable to believe that if we restore the used-up mineral and organic matter, and if we see to it that there is an adequacy of water and air, the fertility of the soil will continue to maintain itself. The great forests, the huge groves of trees and masses of vegetation which we know exist unaided by man, are growing within the scope of this simple formula—straight, unadulterated mineral matter, organic matter, water, and air. The great redwood trees of the western coast which tower into the clouds depend on nothing more than these four things.

Composition of the Soil

Let us look at the soil, an ideal example being approximately as follows:

Organic matter	5%
Minerals	45%
Water	25%
Air	25%
	100%

Much of our land today, however, due to our system of intensive cropping and failure to replace the used-up organic matter, looks something like this:

Organic matter	1%
Minerals (normal type)	35%
Water	15%
Air	15%
Minerals (abnormal)	34%
	100%

What do we mean by abnormal minerals? They are minerals that are ordinarily present in reasonable amounts but, when chemical fertilizers are employed, pile up in dangerous quantities. A small amount may be desirable; a large quantity may cause trouble, like iodine in the human system.

For example, superphosphate, a common artificial fertilizer, is used for its phosphorous content; but by a chemical process an equal amount of sulphuric acid is put into it, merely to give it the quality of solubility, so that it becomes immediately "available" to a plant as a food. The plant roots, however, are somewhat discriminating. They require a great deal of phosphorous but little of sulphur. Therefore the sulphur content of the soil increases tremendously, adding to the store of abnormal minerals.

There are two separate forces at work in the soil—the chemical and the biological—the latter consisting of living micro-organisms, such as bacteria, fungi, actinomycetes, yeasts, et cetera. The presence of sulphur causes a certain bacteria, the sulphur-reducing type, to work upon it and to break it from its compound form. In doing so, these bacteria, in order to obtain energy, have to feed on organic matter, depleting it seriously. That is one of the reasons, as shown in the last table, why the store of the soil's organic matter could easily become exhausted. Other artificial fertilizers, such as chlorides and soda, also leave unwanted and dangerous chemical residues which act in unexpected ways to hurt the soil. The chlorides reduce the germinating quality of seeds, while the soda, from nitrate of soda, hardens the soil.

Looking again at our first table, which consists of the four items—organic matter, minerals, water, and air—we see the course which is best to follow.

We must dig in plenty of organic matter.
We must use the ground-rock powders for their mineral content.

An adequate supply of organic matter will conserve the water supply.

The organic matter also will aerate the ground, thus providing the necessary quantity of air.

The use of chemical fertilizers hardens the soil, interfering with its stores of water and air.

When we feed the earth only with the elements of which it is naturally constituted, we are not gambling. And since the gardener will soon discover that he can secure a greater harvest of vegetables by following the organic system, he will realize how wrong the chemical method is.

The Subsoil

We have been discussing the soil in its general aspects. Now let us look at the subsoil as distinguished from the topsoil. When we speak of soil fertility we think only of the topsoil. In fact, the average gardener regards the subsoil as some sort of enemy —a calamity when he sees a little of it coming up into the surface layer. He does not consider it much less than a poison and feels that something terrible is going to happen to the plants that are to come. We often hear the term "the unproductive subsoil," but this is a serious misstatement. The soil is a loose and friable material in which plants, by means of their roots, find a foothold and nourishment as well as other conditions for growth. Subsoil is usually not so loose as topsoil, but it provides a medium for the roots to hold, gives nourishment to them, and serves other functions as well.

When all is said and done, it will probably be found that the subsoil is of equal importance to the topsoil, which reminds me of a case that came to my attention a few years ago. A man purchased a house and discovered that the grounds had been filled in to a depth of twelve feet with excellent topsoil which had been excavated from the site. His eyes gleamed as he stirred his fingers through the fertile soil. What wonderful plants he would grow with this manna from the heavens! But, alas, he experienced nothing but misfortune with the plants that grew in it. There was disease, oversucculence, and generally poorer results than he was normally accustomed to achieving in his gardening activities. He had overlooked the fact that plants have been bred by Nature for millions of years to have their feet in subsoil. It was as though he were giving them a meal that consisted entirely of dessert.

Micro-organisms

It is interesting to note the variations that exist in the action of topsoil versus subsoil. First we must understand that the micro-organisms—the bacteria and fungi—are far more numerous in the topsoil. Where, in these upper soil levels, they may reach billions per gram of soil. In the subsoil, three feet down, there may be only thirty or forty thousand per gram, in the topsoil the earth is alive with these wrecking crews, for it is there that the plant and animal remains have to be broken down. This is one function that can be performed quickly and efficiently only in the topsoil. Bury a piece of cotton three feet down in soil and it will remain undecayed for a long time. In the topsoil it will disintegrate in a few months.

At the surface, the bacteria are at work synthesizing food. This is another function that goes on at a slower rate of speed in the subsoil, but nevertheless it is an important activity that takes place there. This is a material and valuable source of mineral food for crops. It is interesting to note the means used for transferring some of this mineral matter into plants. The earthworm is one agent that performs this task. It burrows in the subsoil, eating some of it as it goes, bringing it up to the surface and depositing it there in the form of castings. This should give some enterprising manufacturer an idea. Here is an opportunity for him to put on the market a tool which can take tiny amounts of subsoil from three to four feet below the surface without disturbing the topsoil. At those depths there is less likelihood of the existence of mineral deficiencies. This practice might be especially desirable if one has put too much compost into the topsoil.

Function of the Roots

The roots of trees perform a similar function to that of the earthworms, but in a different manner. Some tree roots descend to depths of twenty feet or more and bring into their leaves a rich store of minerals, so that when the leaves fall and decay they deposit a precious treasure on the topsoil. The roots of some ordinary crops go much deeper than suspected and are able to draw in mineral sustenance from low subsoil levels. In 1945 Rodale Press published a booklet (now out of print)— a condensation of the Weaver and Bruner book (also out of print) *Root Development of Vegetable Crops* (McGraw-Hill, 1927)—which gives amazing examples of plant root depths. An illustration demonstrating some astonishing facts is reproduced herewith:

One of the advantages of such large root-systems is that when the plant dies the roots are "eaten up" by the soil (subsoil as well as topsoil) and furnish much fertilizer value. These roots are extremely rich in nitrogen, phosphorus, and potash as well as the trace-mineral elements. In the case of a stand of two-year-old clover, over three tons per acre of roots were left in the soil as a residue. This residue contained 180 pounds of nitrogen, 71 pounds of phosphoric acid, and 77 pounds of potash. It is interesting to note that there is a greater abundance of roots in plants growing by the organic method. This has been proven so conclusively that there can be no question as to its accuracy. This amounts to significant additional poundage of dead roots per acre as food for future crops.

We may add also that roots, as they penetrate into the subsoil, make long holes which provide drainageways for moisture. Here again, by the organic method, there are more and wider holes. Between the earthworms' burrowings and the roots' penetration, a refractory subsoil can be kept adequately open.

The Mycorrhiza

Since there are fewer bacteria at the lower levels to aid the roots in gathering food, Nature has found other means of performing this task. The root hairs themselves are active in drawing in nutriment from the soil's water solution. But we must not overlook the function of the mycorrhiza, a fungus which grows on many plant roots and which lives in a symbiotic relationship with them: that is, each giving something to the other. The mycorrhiza is enabled to live while it transforms substances from the soil into a food for the roots. Eventually the entire mycorrhiza is consumed by the roots as food. Experiments have shown that where chemical fertilizers are used, the mycorrhiza is either absent or very little exists, and it is not absorbed into the plant. In a healthy mycorrhizal association, humus is needed as part of the food picture. This subject is mentioned here because thus far in the literature of the organic method the point has not been stressed. In fact, it has not even been mentioned. In other words, the mycorrhiza may be the specific vehicle to operate at subsoil levels where there is a dearth of other biologic life such as bacteria, fungi, et cetera. Also it may be the means of absorbing minerals from those levels.

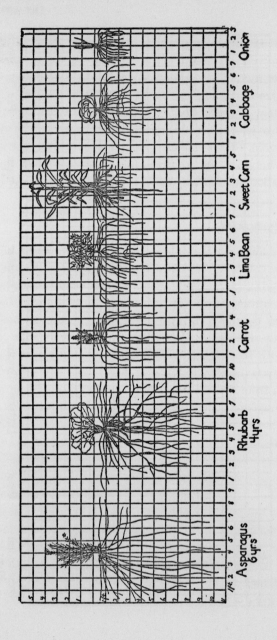

Asparagus 6yrs   Rhubarb 4yrs   Carrot   Lima Bean   Sweet Corn   Cabbage   Onion

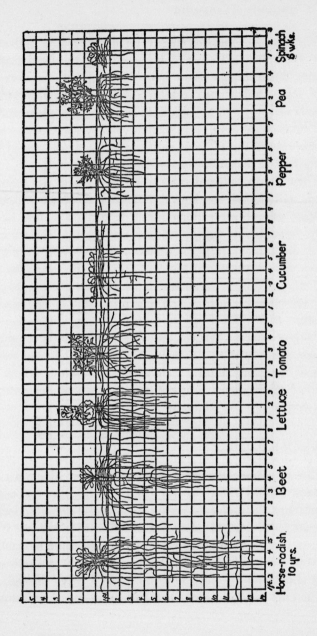

We must not think that there is no organic matter in the subsoil. We know that some of it comes from the dead roots of plants. Some leaches down from the topsoil by the action of rain water. Millar and Turk, in a study of organic matter in topsoil as compared to subsoil, in their book *Fundamentals of Soil Science* (Wiley), state that the amount of organic matter in the subsoil varied from 10 per cent to 15 per cent of that in the topsoil, depending on the kind of soil it was.

There are exceptional cases where the subsoil has more organic matter than the topsoil, but these are freak situations.

Most subsoils are extremely rich in mineral matter, having been formed from the parent rock underneath. The minerals, then, are formed quite far down in the soil, and the farther down you go, the more abundant they are. But since the subsoil mineral content varies widely in different regions, *why not use subsoil material from one region as a soil amendment for another, to be placed into its topsoil!* This would be one way to correct mineral deficiencies. The Chinese make a practice of spreading canal and river mud over their soils; but this, of course, is mostly topsoil rich in organic matter which has washed off their land. Why not go a step further, however, and dig deeper for more minerals?

Mineralize Your Soil

Our experimental farm is located between Allentown and Emaus, Pennsylvania, in the Lehigh Valley. In the nearby Pennsburg, Pennsylvania, region is a mineral-rich red soil which is most fertile. An old inhabitant of that section tells me it is a known fact that the farmers who farmed on these red soils all became rich, while those on the neighboring brown soils were just about able to make ends meet. As I drive through this section my mouth waters when I see piles of red soil, dug up out of excavations for new houses, that will soon be hauled away to dumps or used for non-agricultural fill-ins. What a wonderful soil amendment this would be for the neighboring brown soils! Gardeners should travel with some kind of basket or tin, so that they could gather up some of this unwanted soil to augment the mineral needs of their topsoil.

Westward from our farm is the gravelly, shale soil region which is potato-growing country. A mixture of this shale subsoil with that of the Pennsburg red would be just what the doctor ordered for our soil, which is called Hagerstown clay loam— a heavy clay soil which could stand a little "opening" as well as enriching.

Some of the arid desert soils of western United States are terrifically rich in minerals because there is not sufficient rainfall to leach them down to the water table. Irrigation usually makes such soils blossom with luxuriant crops. The government could very well ship out some of these subsoils by the carload to neighboring farm lands as a subsidy. They do it now in the case of lime and other fertilizer materials.

Years ago, on a cross-country train, I met a party consisting of some Britishers who were visiting this country. As we were going through some dry desert sections of New Mexico, one of them commented on the barrenness of the soil. I explained to him that this was not so, that were it not for a lack of water, the land would pour out a lavish abundance of crops. Just as I spoke we passed a small pond of water. The land surrounding it was made up of the same type of arid soil, but there was a grove of large, sturdy, rich-looking trees growing there. The visitors saw the point at once.

Mixing Subsoil and Topsoil

The question is, what will the addition of subsoil do to a top-

soil? Will it "spoil" it in any way? Will it slow down its ability
to produce a satisfactory crop? The answer is, I believe, that
it must be done judiciously. I would say that in an average
garden a layer of about a half inch of subsoil well mixed into
the upper six inches could be taken in its stride by the soil. If
your soil is well supplied with organic matter, which means
that it is abundant with bacteria and fungi, the first rain will
wash the organic matter into the new material and go to work
on it. In a few days it will thoroughly saturate every pore space
of it and thus begin to break down its rawness. The gardener
can help the process along by watering.

Weir, in his book *Soil Science: Its Principles and Practice*
(Lippincott), says that even if large quantities of raw subsoil
are plowed up to the surface, it probably will become sufficiently weathered before planting time. There are cases, however, where a farmer has plowed too soon after a rain, and the
subsoil has been churned up in big, undigestible, cloddy lumps,
which will surely lead to trouble. Weir says further, "Hilgard
(1892), observing normal growth of vegetables on some desert
soil material that had been excavated from depths of from
seven to ten feet, concluded that subsoils of arid regions gave
no evidence of infertility known as 'rawness.' C. B. Lipman
(1917) has observed that arid subsoils are but little, if at all,
less raw than those of soils of humid regions. . . . In his discussion of this problem, Alway (1918) has stated that the generally accepted ideas regarding the rawness of subsoil materials
in humid regions is not based on pot experiments. . . ."

Actually, as you can see, very little is known about the action of the subsoils in growing plants. Here is a tremendous
field for research. There are regions that contain many soils
which are oversupplied with organic matter but which are lacking in minerals. Such lands exist in Michigan, in the Everglades
of Florida, and in other regions. They should do well with

copious additions of mineral-rich subsoils from other sections which could be quarried on a commercial scale. Heavy clay soils can be aerated by such augmentations, while very sandy soils could be "plugged" with clayey subsoil material. All that is needed in some research and the development of a proper material-handling equipment which would not make the cost prohibitive.

Here is an opportunity for a new industry. I can see a company which stocks twenty-nine different subsoil materials, put up in neat packages, each with its printed mineral analysis on it. The gardener sends in a sample of some of his soil from the upper and lower levels, and the company, after analyzing it, suggests three or four different subsoils for him to purchase. Perhaps someone will do this someday! There is no charge for the idea, and no patents. I wish to stress here that too many organic gardeners have been working to their own disadvantage and have produced an unbalanced soil. They have piled prodigious amounts of organic matter into it, and have neglected the mineral side. Of course they are using the rock powders—the phosphate, potash, basalt, lime, et cetera—but here is a different, new conception of achieving soil fertility. I hope it will be given some consideration.

ORGANIC MATTER

Organic matter is a substance that is alive or that was once living. In the biologic field the dictionary will define the word *organic* as pertaining to, or deriving from, anything that has life. The only known substances that are alive are in plants, animals, and man. Among the lower forms of plants we find bacteria or molds. Incidentally, many persons believe that germs are tiny animals. This is not so. They are bacteria or molds, which are lower forms in the plant world. People confuse them with protozoa, which are one-celled animals.

In the upper seven inches of an acre of soil the weight of bacteria might average four to eight hundred pounds. Besides the protozoa in the soil there are other lower forms of animal life, such as nematodes and rotifers. The functioning of both lower-form groups—that is, plant as well as animal—provides considerable amounts of organic matter.

Organic matter also represents the remains of all kinds of plants and animals in various stages of decomposition. Typical examples are leaves, weeds, grass clippings, sawdust, manure, the bodies of cows or pigs, bacteria, et cetera. A piece of stone would not usually be referred to as organic matter, although in extremely rare cases rock may be found that does contain some. A piece of cotton or woolen cloth might be termed organic matter, the way we usually use the term, because it comes from a plant and animal respectively, although it usually has some inorganic minerals included in its make-up. Dirt as swept up from a floor is usually a combination of organic and inorganic material. Hair is organic. Metallic iron is inorganic. Substances such as calcium, phosphorus, and sulphur are inorganic. However, all organic matter has some inorganic matter in its make-up.

Green Matter

The term *green matter* differs from organic matter in that it includes only plant materials. It is applied to any plant matter, whether it is freshly cut and green or older stuff. It may consist of fresh or withered lawn clippings or weeds, dry leaves, cured hay, or sawdust.

Mold

The term *mold* is often used in the expression *leaf mold*. According to the dictionary, it is a soft, rich soil of an earthy material. The word *molder* means to crumble by natural decay, and that is exactly what happens to leaves that fall and which are not removed by man. They decompose into a form of compost which is called *leaf mold*.

These terms indicate a vast array of decomposable materials which are in the category of organic matter. They include city garbage, leather dust of shoe factories, cannery wastes, apple pomace of cider mills (skins), spoiled milk, and hundreds of other types. Much of this material today is wasted. By proper handling and quick decomposition processes, they could be turned into valuable organic, humus-containing fertilizers.

Total Organic Matter

Sometimes we use the term *total organic matter* to refer to organic materials in general, reserving the term *humus* for the real organic fraction of it which is realized when the process of decomposition goes into action.

Compost

The specialized meaning of the word *compost* as it applies to farming and gardening, according to Webster's New International Dictionary, Second Edition, Unabridged, is, *"A mixture for fertilizing or renovating land in which plants are grown; now, esp., a fertilizing mixture composed of such substances as peat, leaf mold, manure, lime, etc., thoroughly mingled and decomposed, usually in a heap called a compost heap."* This is not a bad definition, but it is not the best. The important thing to note is that the material must be decomposed in order to be called compost. There are two basic things about a compost heap: it must have organic materials, and it must have the proper conditions to make them decompose. The degree of decomposition may be referred to in terms such as *finished* or *unfinished compost*. In a finished compost the material is judged by the reduction of its fibrous appearance.

In an agricultural textbook you may find the following type of definition: "A compost is a fertilizing mixture of partially decomposed organic materials of plant or animal origin, or both, and may include substances such as ash, lime, and chemicals." In the organic method we would exclude the ash, if it is from coal, and would also condemn the addition of the usual fertilizing chemicals.

In review we can see that organic matter is the raw material of the composting process which results in the formation of humus. Composting, then, is a process of making humus.

Carbon and Carbon Compounds

The term *organic* has several meanings. It may be used, as we have said, to denote matter that is living or that was once alive, or it may be used to denote anything containing carbon. All organic matter contains carbon, but there is a class of carbon-containing compounds which we would not consider a type of organic material usable as a fertilizer. One of them is petroleum. Impregnate your soil with this oil and you will destroy its ability to raise crops for a long time.

There is an entire field of chemistry devoted to the study of this type of organic substance, or carbon compounds, some of which are known to cause cancer. For a long time a yellow organic color pigment, called *butter yellow*, was used to color butter. It was banned by the government a few years ago when experiments proved that it caused cancer. Other examples of organic compounds of this type are alcohol and many coal-tar derivatives, such as aspirin, synthetic vitamins, et cetera. In our consideration of organic materials which are used by organiculturists, we must completely exclude these chemical carbon compounds.

About 50 per cent of organic matter is made up of carbon. All carbohydrates, for example, contain a lot of it. Carbon rarely exists alone, as it does in a diamond, which is pure carbon. In coal or charcoal, in graphite or in a plant, it is in compound form. In limestone it is in the form of calcium carbonate;

in washing soda it is sodium carbonate. You can eat calcium carbonate—it is given to babies in the form of limewater—but if you were to consume sodium carbonate you would not live long.

In the air and in the soil, carbon is found in the form of carbon dioxide—CO_2—a gas consisting of one atom of carbon and two of oxygen. It is a colorless and odorless gas which is used in making carbonated soft drinks. When one atom combines with only one atom of oxygen we have CO, carbon monoxide, a violent poison which comes from the exhaust of automobiles.

Carbon dioxide is present in the air to the extent of only .03 per cent, which means three parts out of ten thousand, but its presence in the atmosphere is absolutely necessary for the existence of man, plant, and animal. Without it, life would come to an end. It is the source from which the plant gets its carbon for the energy it needs in order to grow.

Carbon dioxide is a very heavy gas. Therefore, in a silo, where the fermenting matter is giving it off constantly, there is danger of suffocation if a person enters without first leaving the doors wide open so that the gas can escape. Being heavy, it accumulates at the bottom of the silo.

The Carbon Cycle

As we have pointed out, when organic matter decays, carbon dioxide is given off. This process is the basis of life itself, for the gas goes into the soil atmosphere and is used again by growing plants through their leaves. This is known as the carbon cycle. In this cycle not only does carbon dioxide come from decaying organic matter but also from the respiration of plant roots. Some of it is also brought down in rain water. For many years it was believed that plants secured their carbon only from the atmosphere, but in 1924 Lundegradh discovered that decaying organic matter in the soil was a more important source. Modern gardening, however, with its accent on chemical fertilizers and the neglect of the maintenance of adequate supplies of organic matter, reduces the quantity of carbon dioxide in the soil. This may seriously reduce crop yields.

It is known that plants can use much more carbon dioxide than is normally present in air. Recently, in Germany, experiments have been conducted to add carbon dioxide to the air of greenhouses in order to make plants grow better.

We often hear the word photosynthesis in connection with the carbon cycle. This refers to the manufacturing process which goes on in a plant's leaves, which is made possible through the action of sunlight and which takes in the manufacture of plant food from carbon dioxide, water, and other nutrients. Sunlight is the basis of photosynthesis.

Scientific workers have found that the amount of carbon dioxide in a soil is directly dependent on the amount of organic matter present: it rises and falls with it. In fact, the amount of carbon dioxide escaping from soil has been used as a measure of the amount of organic matter present in the soil. In one experiment it was shown that four times as much carbon dioxide was given off from a manured soil as compared to an unmanured soil. The factors that aid in decomposition of organic matter are the same factors that are good for the production of carbon dioxide: namely, high temperature, sufficient moisture, and adequate aeration.

Faulkner's Carbon-Dioxide Ideas

The question is, in regard to the production of carbon dioxide in the soil, which is the better method—composting of organic materials or applying them raw to the soil? In many situations the latter is the better method. I would like to quote from a letter sent me by Faulkner, author of *Plowman's Folly*, a few years ago:

"Composting, unless done with such perfection that none of the gaseous carbon dioxide escapes, must necessarily be less efficient in producing carbonates from the soil—per ton of original organic matter. When raw organic matter is intimately mixed with soil (so intimately that there are no bunches) each fragment is surrounded by soil; and the carbon dioxide it releases immediately finds the minerals upon which it can work; and abundance of plant food carbonates necessarily results. I believe that in this way the maximum effect from a given amount of organic matter is obtained. It is conceivable that equal success might be had by compost methods, but for large areas I feel sure that composting can be no better; besides being laborious as compared with the mere mixing in by machinery of a green manure crop."

From observation and study, I am certain that, in composting, large amounts of carbon dioxide dissipate into the atmosphere because of the heat generated. For this reason an anaerobic form of composting, where as much air as possible is kept from the fermenting matter, will be the means of conserving more of the carbon.

The Effect of Chemical Fertilizers on the Carbon Cycle

The use of chemical fertilizers retards the formation of carbon dioxide for many reasons. Its use results in lower moisture, poorer aeration, and depressions in soil temperature. Tests have shown that a soil high in organic matter will have somewhat higher temperatures. Certain fertilizers, such as nitrate of soda, cause a severe hardening of soils, reducing their aeration —and good aeration is important so that a sufficient supply of carbon dioxide might be given off. It is a known fact that many farmers who use chemical fertilizers forsake the manure pile and overlook the use and importance of organic matter. Organic gardeners should feel that there is sufficient organic matter in their soils to supply a steady and adequate stream of carbon-dioxide gas.

Just as the plant must have carbon dioxide, so must the micro-organisms of the soil. It furnishes their energy. In fact, the formation of carbon dioxide from organic matter is almost entirely due to the action of bacteria. They make it and use it. The soil bacteria and other micro-organisms also produce carbon dioxide as a waste product of their own metabolism. This is what makes the heat in composting.

A sufficient supply of carbon dioxide in the soil will create a healthy dark green foliage in plants. The abundance of carbon dioxide in soil varies at different seasons. In certain experiments it was found highest in May and in August. This may be a combination of seasons when organic matter decays most readily, plus the time when organic matter is plowed under—added organic matter put in the soil by the farmer, plus crop residues plowed under.

In recent years there has been a tendency to apply carbon black to the soil to give it a darker color for the purpose of raising the soil's temperature. The effect of this form of carbon is not yet fully understood. A higher temperature will cause bacteria to work faster and may increase yields, but it is possible that ingredients of the carbon black, other than carbon, may gradually affect the soil's ability to produce.

FOUR

BACTERIA—THE LITTLE SOIL "WRECKERS"

In the soil there is a whole universe, an amazing but fascinating little world peopled by diverse, multipurposed, micro-organisms. It may be compared to *Alice in Wonderland,* because things are done there by rote and rule different from that to which we are accustomed. Can you picture a man consuming twice his own weight of food in an hour? In that world you will find all kinds of elements—police and thieves, builders and wreckers, scavengers, magicians, and circus performers. As a scientific writer put it, "There you will find complex associative and antagonistic interrelationships." It is the way of life in general. There must be positive and negative, angel and devil, republican and democrat. There must be, in Nature's scheme, bacteria which are ready to cause disease if her rules are broken, and there must be bacteria which prevent disease if you give them half a chance.

As the gardener works his soil he must be cognizant that it is full of micro-organisms. Good tilth and a workable soil structure are the result of the activity of bacteria, which exude a gummy substance, a mucus that binds the soil particles together, gluing fine particles into large masses in such a manner as to give it that exquisite quality which you feel when you run your fingers through good earth. In a soil low in bacteria the particles will not "aggregate" as effectively. This good structure of the soil, caused by the activities of bacteria, prevents it from washing away by rain. It reduces soil erosion. When the gardener plants his seed he must be aware that without the action of bacteria the roots cannot feed properly and he cannot secure a satisfactory harvest.

One of the most important functions of bacteria, however, is to break down organic matter. When a crop has completed its task of growing, the bacteria go to work on the old roots which are left in the ground, decomposing them completely and transforming them into food for the next set of roots which will take their place. The question may be asked, why do not the bacteria attack live, growing roots? Are there electrified fences around them which scare them off? The answer is "no." But here is the way it works. There are hundreds of different organisms in the soil—each for its own specific purpose. For example, there is one that can extract only nitrogen from the air. Other bacteria are sulphur-working organisms: they are purple in color and can attack only sulphur. Also there are nitrate-working, cellulose-destroying, sugar-and starch-working bacteria.

Bacteria and Nitrogen

Let us look at one type of bacterial function in detail and you will see how skillful is the hand which has created these living specks, and you will marvel at the system under which they live and work. We will look at the nitrogen "metabolism" of the soil, but not in connection with the nitrogen which is obtained or "fixed" from the air by certain bacteria. We will deal with the nitrogen which is in the soil or in plant or animal matter. There is an ordained procedure which must be carefully executed, step by step, before the nitrogen which is in an old piece of cornstalk, for instance, can be transmuted into a form utilizable by plant roots as food.

First nitrogen comes off, in the process of decay, as ammonia, a compound, each molecule of which contains one atom of nitrogen to three of hydrogen (NH_3). There are special bacteria whose sole function it is to extract this nitrogen from the ammonia, but they have absolutely no power or effect over the hydrogen. They are nitrite-working bacteria. Note that at this stage it is *nitrite*, not *nitrate*. When each atom of nitrogen comes forth from the ammonia, through the intervention of the nitrite-working bacteria, it combines with two atoms of oxygen. The formula for nitrite is NO_2. The "union" will not permit these bacteria to do any other work. This is the only job they are made for. But since the plant roots cannot use nitrogen in the nitrite form (it is very poisonous), another type of bacteria has to come into the picture—the nitrate-working bacteria. They turn the nitrite into the nitrate form, which means that they push another atom of oxygen into the molecule. Now we have NO_3. That bit of extra oxygen turns it into a more or less harmless compound and it becomes fit as a plant food.

Under certain conditions, however, the nitrate in the plant becomes unstable—loses one atom of oxygen and turns back into the nitrite form. This is especially prone to happen in the green leafy vegetables, and the bodies of people who consume too much of them may be harmed. Chemistry is peculiar. Take the case of water. It consists of two parts of hydrogen to one part of water. Hydrogen peroxide is one part of hydrogen to one part of water. But if you drank peroxide, you would not be long for this world.

Bacteria and Roots

The function of some bacteria is to clear the soil of the old roots. How do they know the exact moment when the roots die so that they can begin to do their work? It's the same old story. There are certain bacteria whose only function it is to break down dead matter. Anything alive is distasteful to them. They are wreckers. I was thinking of them a few weeks ago as I walked down Broadway in New York City, near Houston Street. A whole square block of old office buildings was in the process of being razed to make way for a new structure. It was a huge project. The men working at various sections of it seemed like tiny, moving specks. From a distance, to me they were the saprophytic bacteria—those who destroy dead matter. They were divided into groups. Some only took things apart. Others were concerned with separating the different elements or components into usable groups to be shipped elsewhere and applied in building other structures.

In the soil the saprophytic bacteria decompose the old roots into substances which are worked over by other organisms and transformed into food for the plants. One of the important functions of soil bacteria, then, is to provide plants with food. Therefore, if the farmer and gardener can so regulate their methods as to consider the well-being of the micro-organisms of the soil, so that they can multiply to abundance, he will be well repaid for his efforts. To illustrate one aspect of the advantage of a bacteria-rich fertility: if there is a lack of bacteria when a crop of corn is harvested and the heavy stalks plowed under, a temporary indigestion will occur which will reduce the yield of the next crop. That is, any organic matter that has been placed in the soil will not decay.

This principle is illustrated by an experiment described in *The Living Soil* (Lady Eve Balfour, Devin-Adair Co.). Two different soils were taken—one from a field where chemical fertilizers were used, and the other from a soil rich in organic matter (the latter, of course, having a much higher bacterial count). In each batch of soil a piece of cotton wool was dug in. After four months the piece of cotton wool in the chemicalized soil had decayed about 10 per cent whereas that in the organic-matter-rich plot was over 91 per cent consumed. As you already may have guessed, there were much more bacteria in the organically treated soil, and it was their work which disintegrated the cotton wool so fast.

If you were to throw a gunny sack on top of a soil it would be completely decomposed in a certain length of time, depending on how rich the soil is in bacteria. If an organic gardener were to do this, he would find that it might take about a year. But if the sack were to be placed on the land of a gardener using chemical fertilizers and applying little organic matter, it might take two or even three years. And if the sack were dug *into* the soil, the decomposition would take place much faster, because bacteria work faster with better conditions of warmth and moisture.

Biologic Health of Soil

In organic gardening we give a thought to the maintenance of the biologic state of health of the little world that exists in the soil. We keep a microbial force working for us that is ready to go to work instantly on any raw organic matter or inert mineral parts of the soil—to make them available as plant food. We learn with gratification, when we begin to secure much higher crop yields than our neighbors, how valuable these microscopic wrecking crews are. In addition, the dying bodies of these microbes give us a significant amount of protein-rich fertilizer every year. This reminds me of a story. Once I was part of a group of spectators held spellbound by a hatless, coatless, sleeveless gentleman on a Philadelphia street corner who was selling a health book. He said, "And what, may I ask, do you accomplish by boiling your water, in order to sterilize it? You kill the germs! So you're drinking dead germs!" I don't think there is any medical proof that there is danger in drinking water with dead germs in it, but we do know that dead germs in the soil are greatly appreciated by live roots.

In agriculture the dead bacteria, the "germs" that die a natural death, provide a significant amount of food for crops. Their dead bodies contain a wonderfully rich organic matter full of valuable proteins, minerals, and other highly desirable nutritional elements. If the gardener would follow the kind of practices that multiply his bacteria, it would be like the setting up of an annuity, the provision for a recurring, dependable income on which he could lean from year to year, very much like coupons on a bond or money in a bank.

Bacteria, if understood properly and harnessed in the right way, can help the gardener in many ways. They can inactivate larvae of dangerous, disease-producing insects by getting at them at the source—in the soil. They can be a factor in getting more food for crops from organic and inorganic stores of it in the soil.

Antibiotic Aspects of Soil

There is one aspect of the little microbiological world in the soil which is amazing. It carries its own police force. You have heard of penicillin. Perhaps you have had the use of it. Well, penicillin is an organic substance excreted by the penicillum mold, which is a micro-organism closely related to bacteria, although usually somewhat larger in size. There is a large family of antibiotic organisms, of which penicillin is only one. Streptomycin, terramycin, and many others are in this group, which have been in the soil since time began. They are protective devices of Nature—little policemen that are in the soil to keep the disease-producing, bandit organisms from getting out of hand. They lull them and keep them inactivated by excretions from their bodies.

We know from experience that in gardens where conditions in the soil are kept as natural as possible—that is, withholding from the soil all strong chemicals and poison sprays—there will be few signs of disease in plants, thanks to these antibiotic organisms. Under these conditions this type of micro-organism is in good supply, in vigorous health, and in a position to regulate competently the life that goes on below ground.

The large drug firm of Charles Pfizer and Company, in Brooklyn, is aware that in searching for new antibiotic organisms they will have little success if they look in soils where chemical fertilizers have been consistently employed, as strong chemicals will kill off some of the antibiotic organisms and decrease the effectiveness of others. So they wrote some time ago, asking us if we would give them the names of several thousand of the readers of *Organic Gardening* magazine so that they could write each one asking for a small sample of their soil. We gave them the names and they wrote the letters, but they did not inform us as to whether they secured any results. That is probably a deep trade secret. However, it is a good tip for other drug companies.

There can be no question that many chemical fertilizers and insecticides kill off the antibiotic organisms of the soil, thus permitting disease-producing organisms to become more active.

There is a growing tendency to depend on poison sprays to do the job of controlling disease. But the more chemicals are used, the more they seem to be required. Organisms develop tolerances to the poisons, and new ones come to complicate matters.

Even if you are only a gardener, be aware that all of this knowledge applies to your soil, to your vegetables, and to your flowers. By nursing along and encouraging the micro-organisms in the soil, by feeding them sufficient quantities of the kind of food they prefer—namely, living organic matter and the mineral rock powders—and shunning strong chemicals in any form, you will develop a much finer soil, and your results will show it. Besides, in the beginning as well as in the long run, it is cheaper.

FIVE

EARTHWORMS AND THEIR IMPORTANCE TO THE GARDENER

The earthworm is a valuable adjunct in the soil's expression of fertility. He digests the soil—eats it and conditions it. Our topsoils have practically been made by earthworms. That is why Aristotle called them the intestines of the soil. Their castings are far richer minerally than the soil which they ingest. It is said that an average earthworm will produce its weight in castings every twenty-four hours. They burrow into the ground, as far as six feet down, aerating the soil, making holes for rain to penetrate. They break up hardpans which have been created by chemical fertilizers and other artificial horticultural practices. Each year their dead bodies furnish a considerable amount of valuable nitrogenous fertilizer, which may amount to more than a thousand pounds per acre in a highly "organic soil." Organic matter and mineral rock fragments are their natural food. The gardener should use no other fertilizers, for if he does, he will be destroying a very valuable ally.

Jack Offerman, western vice-president of the American Delphinium Society, had an unpleasant experience with earthworms affected by a chemical fertilizer. On April 25, 1947, he wrote us: "One morning, strolling through my garden, I found to my distress a great number of earthworms all dead, laying on the surface of one of the new beds. These worms looked as though they had eaten poison. Later in the day I found out that my helper had mixed the soil with commercial fertilizer the night before. I knew there was only a small amount of commercial fertilizer in store, but it was sufficient to kill a great number of worms in a bed four feet by eighty feet long. Since this incident occurred, there will be no more commercial fertilizer used in my garden; the result in growing my delphiniums with compost has been far over my expectation."

I know that in the irrigation systems in California the application of liquid ammonia fertilizers which are high in nitrogen causes earthworms to come to the surface and die there immediately.

Sir Albert Howard and Other Organic Gardeners on the Earthworm

Sir Albert Howard, in the introduction to *Darwin on Humus and the Earthworm* (Faber & Faber, Ltd.), said: "In following the ploughs in the autumn and spring in the Spalding area, I always found that where heavy dressings of artificials were used every year, with or without organic matter, earthworms were rare. I sometimes walked half a mile after the ploughs and cultivators without seeing one."

In the *Gippsland and Northern Co-Operator* of June 14, 1945, published in Melbourne, Australia, an experience of Percy G. Weston with the use of superphosphate as a fertilizer is recorded. "When these flats were ploughed twenty years ago,"

Mr. Weston says, "they simply teemed with millions of worms. Now the plough reveals that this great friend of man has vanished or is fast vanishing." In Mr. Weston's case he had row crops from time to time in his rotation, crops such as corn, tobacco, and tomatoes.

Peter D. Barakauskas, teacher of horticulture at the Henry Ford School of Vocational Guidance in Agriculture and Industry, wrote me, "My repeated greenhouse tests with earthworms and fertilizers have showed the opposite results that they claim (the opposition). Earthworms have disappeared from the fertilizer pots, while they have multiplied in unfertilized ones."

Poison Sprays and Earthworms

Again Sir Albert Howard says in the same introduction quoted above: "The use of artificial manures is not the only modern practice which destroys the earthworms. Hardly less injurious are the poison sprays such as Bordeaux mixture and other powders containing copper salts, tar oils, and the lime-sulphur washes used for the control of insect pests. Perhaps the most complete account of such results is that given by Dreidax in the *Archiv fur Pflanzenbau*, 7, 1921, and in *Rationelle Landwirtschaft*, Wilhelm Andermann, Berlin, 1927. The first of these papers concludes with a long list of references dealing among other matters with investigations on the earthworm since *The Formation of Vegetable Mold* by Darwin was published in 1881. In the latter work Dreidax sums up his observations on the deleterious effects of poison sprays on the earthworm population of vineyards in Germany.

"While examining a vineyard situated in the Markgraf near Auggen in south Baden, in which poison sprays were constantly used, he found a surprising fall from the abundant earthworm population of meadows and orchards under grass adjoining the vineyard to that of the vineyard itself. The growth of the vines always corresponded closely with the number of earthworms: the rows next to the grass border were well developed: the vines in the centre of the vineyard, where there were no earthworms, did badly. In this investigation the earthworm population under the grass border invariably stopped dead wherever poison sprays reached the turf.

"A visit to almost any orchard in Kent during the spring immediately after the trees are sprayed with tar oils or lime sulphur will be sufficient to prove how harmful this spraying is to the earthworm population. The ground soon afterwards is covered with a carpet of dead worms."

I would like to present a letter from a reader of *Organic Gardening*, but the name is omitted for obvious reasons:

"When I was a beginning gardener, I used to call the Field Station very frequently for help and information. They were very helpful and friendly.

"Four years ago I began to work with Hybrid Earthworms and the next year I saw an article by Professor —— making considerable fun of the earthworm fad, and showed very little knowledge of the worms' anatomy. I used to teach Biology and have dissected hundreds of them.

"So I immediately phoned Professor —— and asked him how long since he had dissected an earthworm. Then I told him I had been working with them only a year and they seemed to be more than living up to the claims for them. I said I was frankly experimenting and had planted trial plots of tomatoes, lettuce, and peppers with worms and without them for comparison.

"I asked him if he would like a report at the end of the summer, and he said he would. So at the close of the season (1948 drought) I reported to him that despite the weather everything that had the worms was better than I had ever grown—peppers and lettuce were twice as big a crop while the plots that had no worms were hardly worth harvesting—especially the lettuce. Later, I made other brief reports. The next year I sent several samples of soil before the earthworms were added and the same soil one year later. The results really astonished him. My soil is largely gravel. One sample analyzed—no nitrogen, medium low phosphorus, low calcium, low potash, and much aluminum. One year after, one whole box of worms were added and kept heavily mulched with green matter and dried leaves, the analysis was—high nitrogen, very high phosphorus, high potash, and no aluminum. The professor was always interested though slightly skeptical, and when I reported that for the first time in years I had no corn borers, no Mexican bean beetles, no squash bugs, and very few other insects and went the whole season without either spraying or dusting, he laughed." This must have been his way of indicating defeat.

This is very important information, because under certain conditions aluminum can be highly toxic to plants.

The Earthworm and Fungi

There is evidence that earthworms consume eggs of harmful insects in the soil, but an amazing bit of research indicates that they are a regulating factor in the case of damaging fungi. The details of this experiment can be found in Science, March 1952, page 61–87. There was difficulty in breeding T deliensis (Walch) because a fungal mycelis grew in the rearing tubes. Copper-sulphate solution was used in an attempt to control it, with only partial success. In one of the tubes, however, in which a fresh batch of river sand which contained some earthworms had been placed, there was no growth of fungus. "We have since fully convinced ourselves," says the report, "that these earthworms are mainly responsible for keeping down fungal growth." The laboratory then began to collect worms in tubes, putting in mosquito eggs, decaying leaves, rotting filter paper, and other similar substances as food, and found that the earthworms tended to congregate around a clump of mosquito eggs. The encouragement of conditions in the soil that cause earthworms to multiply might be highly desirable in regions over-supplied with mosquitoes.

Breeding Earthworms

In recent years the breeding of earthworms has become a very popular pastime among gardeners, for this reason: earthworms make wonderful compost which they produce in the breeding boxes. There is a special type of breeding earthworm called the *brantling*, which is a manure-pile worm and which is sold by breeders. There are many advertisers in *Organic Gardening* magazine who have such earthworms for sale, and along with the earthworms they usually furnish full details on how to raise them.

These earthworms can be propagated in your compost heap, in outdoor cement pits, or in any kind of wooden box. Usually the boxes or pits are filled with a combination of soil, peat moss, all kinds of organic-matter residues, manure, et cetera.

Earthworms will eat practically anything, but they do have certain definite needs. They must have a good supply of protein. Nitrogenous green matter, raw peanuts, ground-up beans, wheat, or barley will supply this. Some raisers give them a ration of chicken mash regularly. They can get their potash ration from a little cottonseed meal or even from small quantities of wood ash. Sugar, molasses, and coffee grounds provide needed elements. In general, however, practically anything you can eat is good food for an earthworm—plus leaves, grass clippings, and weeds. Some worm ranchers even feed their "live-stock" Pablum!

Earthworms are not fussy. The excellent results obtained from the different breeding and feeding methods suggested by the various breeders is ample proof that anyone can raise earthworms. Give them plenty of food, keep them warm (in the North they must be moved indoors during the winter), provide moisture and shade, and the average commercial worm will produce more humus and baby worms than you would expect.

HUMUS—ITS APPEARANCE AND CHARACTER

Humus is organic matter which is in a more advanced state of decomposition than compost in its early stages. It is usually a dark brown to black color and has decomposed by a process in which microbial and chemical action were factors. In a compost heap some of the organic matter has turned to humus, but the remaining fraction will completely decompose after it is placed in the soil. Organic matter in the soil, in the early stages of decomposition, cannot be called humus. It must still be called organic matter. The process by which organic matter turns to humus is called *humification*.

The great noticeable difference between humus and organic matter is that the latter is rough-looking material, such as coarse plant matter, while in the humus form we find something that has turned into a more uniform-looking substance.

Humus is a heterogeneous complex aggregate which represents a mixture of a large number of different compounds. Although it is extremely variable and heterogeneous, it has its own well-defined characteristics which differ widely from other natural organic substances. It varies according to the origin of its organic matter. In early chemical research on the subject, certain acids under the general classification of humic acids were vaguely referred to as composting humus without much scientific foundation. Fantastic names were given to them. But practically all of this work has been discredited.

Organic and Inorganic Matter in Combination

It is a strange fact that both organic matter and humus always contain inorganic matter. There is really no clear line of demarcation between organic and inorganic matter. In Nature, evidently, organic is never separated from inorganic because one complements the other. They no doubt exert a sort of mutual catalytic action upon each other, and probably take part together in both chemical and biological actions.

The ash of humus consists of major and minor elements. If we remove the major ones, such as calcium, phosphorus, potash, iron, sulphur, we will find only the very tiniest fraction left: the trace-mineral elements—manganese, zinc, copper, iodine, tungsten, molybdenum, et cetera. But we know how important each and every one is, even though it is present in only two or three parts per million of matter. For example, if there is a manganese deficiency, tomato and bean plants will be dwarfed. A lack of zinc will produce mottled leaves on citrus trees. A lack of copper will lower the sugar content of beets.

The process of decomposition from organic matter to humus is one of microbial and chemical action. The microbial process may be referred to as a biological one and includes action of bacteria, fungi, yeasts, algae, actinomycetes, protozoa, enzymes, and so forth. The chemical action comprises hydrolysis (a chemical reaction produced by decomposition of a compound, its elements taking up those of water), oxidation, and reduction (separating of an element from other elements combined with it). In this process, simple compounds are formed which can function directly or indirectly as nutrients. In organic matter, before its decomposition, there is nothing that can feed a plant.

The humus eventually becomes oxidized to carbonic acid, water, nitric acid, and other simple substances serving as food for plants. In the process of humification, the substances are undergoing decomposition, but true humus consists of those portions of the original organic matter which are resistant to further decomposition.

Color of Humus

Humus is the material that usually gives the soil its rich dark color. You will never see light-colored humus. It would be interesting to study the process that goes on within organic matter to make it turn dark when it becomes transformed to humus, but we know that the degree of darkness depends on the character of the organic matter and the length of the decomposition.

The chemical explanation is that in the plant and in the animal the chemical compounds are very complicated, but as the matter turns to humus these compounds resolve themselves into simpler ones. It is from the colors of these simple compounds that the ultimate darkness of humus is achieved. The extent of the color is in proportion to the extent of the decomposition, and the resulting extent of the exposure, so to speak, of these simpler compounds with their characteristic colors. The longer the decomposition, usually, the darker the color becomes. Nature seems to hold a paintbrush and mix colorful pigments. When the yellow of sulphur mixes with the black of carbon, a lighter black or dark brown might result. When you look at humus, or its effect in the soil, bear in mind that what you see is a mixture of ten or twenty or more simple compounds which are contributing their colors to the mixture.

In a plant the green chlorophyll masks the other colors while it is alive, but when it dies and the chlorophyll is dissipated, the colors of the other compounds can show through as soon as a little decomposition takes place. This is what happens to leaves in the autumn. The reds and browns that seem to appear all of a sudden were there all the time, but were masked by the chlorophyll and were lost to view because they were part of more involved compounds. As soon as they "decompose" into simpler compounds, they show their color.

A widely prevalent fallacy about the darkness of humus is that it is due to the presence of a large amount of carbon. Since coal is black and it contains a large amount of carbon, one jumps to the conclusion that carbon is always black. Actually, carbon has a wide range of colors. For example, diamonds are pure carbon and can be yellow, blue, green, pink, et cetera. Carbon in the air is colorless.

The process of darkening in the gradual transition of organic matter to humus can be illustrated by the manufacture of paper pulp from wood. The wood is first reduced in size to chips which are treated with chemical solutions. The wood chips and the cooking liquor mixtures are heated under pressure. As the process proceeds, the liquor assumes darker and darker colors. This is due to the degradation of the lignin and the cellulose, in part, into simpler substances, closely resembling humus, which are in fact identical in chemical composition and structure with humus.

As we have already stated, the dark color depends on the simple compounds which are resolved out of the complex ones, but these depend on the nature of the organic matter from which the humus originates. Very little is known about this except that the dark colors arise mainly from the lignin, tannin, and protein compounds. For example, therefore, if you are making compost from a lot of wheat straw, the resulting humus should be lighter in color than if alfalfa plant matter were used, for the latter is much richer in protein, which means that it contains a large amount of nitrogen. The lignins and tannins contain no nitrogen, being made up solely of hydrogen, oxygen, and carbon. Some people think that the decomposition of animal matter would give a darker humus than that coming from plants, but this is not so. The lignins and tannins of plant matter are also responsible for the dark color factor.

Oxidation—a Factor in Color

Another determinant of color is the extent of the oxidation. The greater the degree of oxidation (and this is related to soil aeration), the lighter the color of any given soil or humus. In the case of soil, where oxygen decreases, black turns to gray while brown turns to yellow.

The tendency of increasing acidity does not necessarily reduce the color of humus, but the addition of lime flocculates the organic matter, reducing the loss of colloidal humus, thus deepening the color.

The use of chemical fertilizers tends to lighten the color of humus. It turns the soil to a grayish color, especially on top.

In review, then, here are the factors which make for the color in humus:

1. Decomposition and reduction to simple compounds.
2. The nature of organic matter from which it originates —the lignin, tannin, and protein making for the darkest colors.
3. The amount of oxidation (aeration).
4. The use of lime.
5. The concentration of chemical fertilizers.

Is the Color of Humus a Clue to the Fertility of the Soil?

It depends on whether the color is due to the humus or to something else that is in the soil, and especially on the age of the humus. Where humus is extremely old, all the usable nutritional elements are out of it, and the mere blackness offers nothing exciting to plants. Old peaty soils are of this character.

Some soils are dark because they may be oversupplied with manganese, others because they may have originated from black rocks, and the dark color may be partly due to weathered rock fragments in the soil. We can safely say that yellow and gray topsoil indicates a soil deficient in humus. Red soils are more productive, the red oxide indicating the presence of iron. In volcanic soils dark-colored minerals will confuse the origin of the darkness. A soil may contain a large supply of old humus in an advanced stage of decomposition and not be as productive as one that is supplied with organic matter that has been applied to it only four or five months ago. The fresh organic matter is also more active in improving the physical condition of the soil. But this organic matter has little influence on soil color.

There are dark peat and muck soils which may be deficient in certain important elements. In the Everglade soils of Florida, which are very dark, a project of raising cabbages many years ago failed because of such deficiency. Today they are using these soils successfully by providing the deficient elements.

Too much blackness in soil, if achieved at the expense of oversupplying the soil with humus, may not be desirable. There is a point beyond which the application of organic matter in gardening may cause actual harm. In farming, however, it is almost impossible to secure that much organic matter. While it is safe to say that in the great majority of situations the darker the soil the more fertile it is, it is wise not to assume that this is always the case.

Temperature and Humus

The darker a substance, the more heat it will absorb. That is why white is worn so frequently in the tropics. A white barn will be cooler inside than one painted red. A darker soil, there-fore, has certain advantages. It may be five or six degrees warmer than a light-colored one. This is of significance in the spring. In a dark-colored soil seeds will germinate earlier and grow faster. This is not mere theory but works out in actual practice. In recent years farmers who have neglected adding organic matter to their soils have taken to applying carbon black for this purpose. In a Canadian experiment in 1941 the yield of cantaloupes was increased by applying black paper to the soil. On the other hand, where crops require a cool tem-perature, farmers have been known to spread a thin film of white chalk on the surface.

Another method of raising the temperature of the soil is to improve its drainage. Too much water in the soil reduces its temperature. This is where the organic method is of great ad-vantage, since the humus prevents waterlogging.

SEVEN

NITROGEN AND ITS IMPORTANCE TO THE SOIL

One of the most important functions of organic matter is to furnish nitrogen. As organic matter decays, nitrogen is set free in a form that is available to plants. The organic gardener can obtain all his minerals from phosphate, potash, and basalt rocks, et cetera, but for him nitrogen is obtainable only in organic matter. Rarely do rocks contain nitrogen. The gardener can also obtain nitrogen from dried blood, bone meal, and tankage as well as from his compost.

Nitrogen is an extremely important element in gardening. Without it, productivity of the soil will decline. High productivity is interrelated with the supply of organic matter in a soil: a deficiency of one usually indicates a deficiency of the other. Nitrogen is necessary to the functioning of every cell of the plant and is needed for rapid growth. It is directly responsible for the vegetative growth of plants above ground. With a good supply of it, maturity of the plant will come earlier.

A lack of nitrogen is indicated by a lightening of the green color of leaves. A great lack of it will show up in the yellowing of the leaves. Of all nutrient deficiencies in arable soils, that of nitrogen is most common. But an excessive supply of it will not only retard the growth period but will reduce the plant's resistance to disease and produce an inferior quality of crop, which will show up in poor keeping and shipping abilities. Too much nitrogen waterlogs the plant, causing an oversucculency. This is where the organic method is superior. The organic matter, unless a tremendous excess is applied to the soil, gradually feeds the nitrogen to the plants as required, rarely overfeeding them. It is a known fact that organic matter decays slowly, thus not releasing the nitrogen too quickly. The organic matter thus is a valuable storehouse of nitrogen, maintaining an automatic supply for the entire growing season. But, as with chemical fertilizers, a too enthusiastic hand can sometimes give the soil an oversupply which will lead to all the troubles described above.

A very common error is found in most agricultural textbooks and publications dealing with the subject of organic matter. The statement is usually made that, on the average, 5 per cent of organic matter consists of nitrogen. This statement bothered me for a long time because I could see from actual analyses of various kinds of organic matter that this could not possibly be true. At the most, organic matter contains up to 2 per cent of nitrogen. Finally the basis of this error dawned upon me. What these agricultural teachers meant was that *humus* contained 5 per cent nitrogen. But there is a big difference between organic matter and humus. It is because of a loose and careless handling of the terms *organic matter* and *humus* that this error occurs again and again.

To me this seems most amazing. To see scientific organizations repeating this gross error is hard to understand. When you start out with a corncob, which is one example of organic matter, you may have something which contains, let us say, less than one half of one per cent nitrogen, but when it has decayed thoroughly and turned to humus, the latter contains 5 per cent of nitrogen. This is brought about by the fact that in the process of decomposition other elements have oxidized on a larger scale than the oxygen. The nitrogen of the corncob for the most part does not dissipate.

The 5-Per-Cent Rule

Here, therefore, is a general rule which I have never seen in any agricultural textbook or publication, but which is true nevertheless. No matter how much or how little nitrogen is in any kind of organic matter to begin with, when it turns to humus the latter's nitrogen content will be about 5 per cent.

The following is a list of representative classifications of organic matter and typical analyses with respect to their nitrogen content:

PLANT WASTES

	% OF NITROGEN
Beet wastes	0.4
Brewery wastes	1.0
Castor pomace	4.0 to 6.6
Cattail reeds	2.0
Cocoa-shell dust	1.0
Cocoa wastes	2.7
Coffee wastes	2.0
Grape pomace	1.0
Green cowpeas	0.4
Nutshells	2.5
Olive residues	1.15
Peanut shells	3.6
Peanut-shell ashes	0.8
Pine needles	0.5

PLANT WASTES CONT.

	% OF NITROGEN
Potato skins	0.6
Sugar wastes	2.0
Tea grounds	4.1
Tobacco stems	2.5 to 3.7
Tung-oil pomace	6.1

LEAVES

Peach leaves	0.9
Oak leaves	0.8
Grape leaves	0.45
Pear leaves	0.7
Apple leaves	1.0
Cherry leaves	0.6
Raspberry leaves	1.35
Garden-pea vines	0.25

GRASSES

Clover	2.0
Red clover	0.55
Vetch hay	2.8
Cornstalks	0.75
Alfalfa	2.4
Immature grass	1.0
Bluegrass hay	1.2
Cowpea hay	3.0
Pea hay	1.5 to 2.5
Soybean hay	1.5 to 3.0
Timothy hay	1.19
Salt hay	1.06
Millet hay	1.22

SEAWEED

Fresh seaweed	0.2 to 0.38
Dry seaweed	1.1 to 1.5

MEAL

Bone-black bone meal	1.5

PLANT WASTES CONT.

	% OF NITROGEN
Raw bone meal	3.3 to 4.1
Steamed bone meal	1.6 to 2.5
Cottonseed meal	7.0
Corn fodder	0.41
Oats, green fodder	0.49
Corn silage	0.42
Gluten meal	6.4
Wheat bran	2.36
Wheat middlings	2.75
Meat meal	9.0 to 11.0
Bone tankage	3.0 to 10.0

MANURES

Cattle manure (fresh excrement)	0.29
Cattle manure (fresh urine)	0.58
Hen manure (fresh)	1.63
Dog manure	2.0
Horse manure (solid fresh excrement)	0.44
Horse manure (fresh urine)	1.55
Human excrement (solid)	1.0
Human urine	0.60
Night soil	0.80
Sheep manure (solid fresh excrement)	0.55
Sheep (fresh urine)	1.95
Stable manure, (mixed)	0.50
Swine manure (solid fresh excrement)	0.60
Swine (fresh urine)	0.43
Sewage sludge	1.7 to 2.26

ANIMAL WASTES
(Other than manures)

Eggshells	1.0
Dried blood	10.0 to 14.
Feathers	15.3
Dried jellyfish	4.6
Fresh crabs	5.0

PLANT WASTES CONT.

	% OF NITROGEN
Dried ground crabs	10.0
Dried shrimp heads	7.8
Lobster wastes	2.9
Shrimp wastes	2.9
Mussels	1.0
Dried ground fish	8.0
Acid fish scrap	4.0 to 6.5
Oyster shells	0.36
Milk	0.5
Wool wastes	3.5 to 6.0
Silkworm cocoons	10.0
Silk wastes	8.0
Felt wastes	14.0

As to the possible reason for the error which exists in the minds of agronomists—that organic matter contains 5 per cent nitrogen, there may be several explanations. First, it may be because of the fact that their work is 99.999 per cent with chemical fertilizers, and although they speak of the need for organic matter in farming, they do not seem to have the desire to convince the typical farmer of its value.

Secondly, it is possible that in the mind of the average agronomist the expression *organic matter* may mean humus. If this is so, it is time we got together on a definition of terms. Perhaps the agronomist, when referring to a specific type of organic matter such as alfalfa hay, may use the term *organic materials* as against *organic matter,* but I think such handling of terms would be confusing. We should consider *humus* as the product that comes into being on the decay of organic matter, and *organic matter* as the specific material which is at the beginning of that process. In other words, the terms *organic matter* and *organic materials* should be considered as one and the same thing.

Nitrogen Compounds

Nitrogen is not present, either in the soil or in humus, in a free condition. If it were, it would be rapidly decomposed by soil organisms and much of it would become lost to growing crops. Nitrogen is present in humus in the form of protein compounds which are highly resistant to microbial dissolution, thus releasing its nitrogen slowly. In raw organic matter, if not carefully handled, much of the nitrogen can become dissipated into the atmosphere in the form of ammonia, which is a compound of nitrogen and which results from the first stage in the breakdown of protein. This is the great value of humus—its ability to hoard its nitrogen for release to plant roots as needed.

Protein

Protein is a different story. It consists of a maximum of six elements: carbon, hydrogen, oxygen, nitrogen, sulphur, and phosphorus. There can be different proportions of each one of these six. Mathematics can be so fantastic that it has been said that over six billion different combinations of these elements are known. In other words, there are more than six billion different kinds of protein. So it is possible for a great variation, and even for a mediocre quality, of protein to creep in here and there. There are delicate relationships in the formation of compounds. For example, water is made up of two parts hydrogen and one part oxygen. In hydrogen peroxide the molecule is made up of the same two elements, but it is a poison. It consists of one atom of hydrogen and one of oxygen. Only one atom of hydrogen less, yet it can kill.

It must be admitted, therefore, that in the possible combinations of the six elements that make up protein there may be some that spell inferior quality.

We can see that protein is like humus. It has no uniform formula, but varies according to how it originated. If it has an artificial chemical origin, it is highly possible that the atoms may arrange themselves differently within the molecule than if the nitrogen is of organic origin. Nature has a way of arranging them, based on an evolution of millions of years. Man, who only recently came upon the scene, cannot hope to duplicate the chemistry of Nature. In fact, no man in any laboratory has ever been able to make protein—even an inferior kind. He has been able to extract nitrogen from the air. But protein is the beginning of life; it is protoplasm, and the making of it is in the hands of a Power higher than man's.

Dr. Selman Waksman, in his book *Humus* (Williams & Wilkins, out of print), item 1082, page 484, cites three researches to show the importance of the nature of protein in the soil in improving its ability to feed plant roots. It would seem logical that, given defective protein, we will have defective plants. In a recent ten-year period in the Middle West the protein content of the grains declined 10 per cent. This is a terrific reduction for such a short period of time. The question is did the quality of the protein also decline? If it did, it might be an explanation for the alarming recent increases in the degenerative diseases, for protein builds body tissue. Defective protein— defective body tissue. Defective body tissue may be more susceptible to cancer.

Nitrogen is important, but the way it is held in the protein molecule may be the one factor which may control the fate of mankind.

I would like to quote Dr. George D. Scarseth, of the American Farm Research Association of Lafayette, Indiana, who in

1947, in a bulletin entitled *Organic Matter and Our Food Supply*, said:

"Protein foods are nitrogen-carrying foods. Every farmer knows that nitrogen and soil organic matter are closely related. Every farmer knows that a soil high in organic matter is also a very productive soil. Every farmer also knows that legumes like clover, alfalfa, and sweet clover add valuable organic matter to the soil. The farmers also know that the organic matter from these legumes is better than the organic matter from non-legumes, because clover makes nitrogen into chemical compounds out of the free nitrogen in the air."

Incidentally, materials high in nitrogen content are extremely important in composting, for nitrogen is the principal food of the bacteria which engage in the decay processes. When the raw materials of composting include highly nitrogenous materials, such as hen manure and alfalfa hay, the composting is accelerated and the quality of the compost better.

Nitrogen and the Dynamic Quality of the Soil

As we have said before, when we place either raw organic matter or what we term finished compost into the soil, decay begins to take place and nitrogen and other substances are released. When there is sufficient organic matter for a continuous process of decomposition to go on, there is always a goodly stream of nitrogen coming from it. There is a dynamic quality, a movement from the organic matter, that is required if it is to be of any value. Were all the organic matter to be applied to the soil in the most advanced stages of decay, there would be no nitrogen available from this source.

Professor Sidney B. Haskell, director of the Massachusetts Agricultural Experiment Station, in his book *Farm Fertility* (Harper, 1923), says:

"The benefit comes not so much from the character of the final product as from the process of decay taking place in the soil itself. Organic matter to be functional in the soil must decay in the soil; and decaying, the supply must be constantly renewed. Otherwise, we either have a barren condition of the soil, brought about by too great a decay of this humus and failure to replace it, or an equally unfavorable condition in which the soil organic matter is dead and inert, like so much peat, or in extreme cases similar in its inertness to coal itself." Thus we have the terms living and dead humus.

A. F. Gustafson, *Nitrogen and Organic Matter in the Soil* (Cornell, March 1941), says:

"It is the newly decomposed organic matter on which crops depend mainly for their nitrogen."

In this publication Mr. Gustafson gives an interesting example of the difference between two soils. An Ontario loam contained 3 per cent organic matter. The Volusia silt loam had 5.2 per cent. Yet the latter, which had about 70 per cent more organic matter, yielded less in crops. The author says that one reason is that the organic matter in the Ontario loam was more active. He states, "Much of that in the Volusia is so inactive that one might regard it as being in a sense embalmed." He advises the liberal addition to it of green manure, leguminous crops, the results of which should not be harvested, but plowed in.

Here we can see that if we wish to produce the most dynamic qualities in the new organic matter, much would depend on the kind of organic matter we plow in. If we put peat into the soil, the dynamic movement of nutrients from it will be very slow. Humus, whether it is in the form of coal or fresh organic matter, represents stored energy, but if it is to be of any value, it must give it off.

Fresh Organic Matter and Nitrogen

It has been found also that when fresh organic matter was added to a soil there was an acceleration in the rate of decomposition of the existing soil organic matter. It probably has something to do with the stimulation of the soil bacteria, somewhat akin to giving them a shot in the arm. In a virgin soil which is first put under the plow the rate of decay of organic matter is very fast at first, but soon it slows down. Evidently the soil bacteria require continued stimulation. This stimulation brings about the dynamic quality that we are discussing.

In the tropics the movement is faster than in the temperate zone, and thus there is always an urgent call for fresh organic matter. The four conditions that make it ideal for micro-organisms to do their share in the processes of decomposition are temperature, moisture, acidity, and aeration. The higher temperatures in the tropics overstimulate bacteria.

Coming back to our general subject, here is an interesting quotation from Edmund L. Worthen's *Farm Soils: Their Management and Fertilization* (John Wiley & Sons, 1941):

"While the fresh, active organic matter content of a soil is an important criterion of its degree of fertility, an unproductive soil may contain a considerable quantity of humus, even enough to produce a dark color. Organic matter in the form of humus contains a smaller proportion of the more essential plant-food elements than does fresh organic matter, and is in such an advanced stage of decomposition that it is very ineffective. It is sometimes referred to as the inactive form of organic matter. It not only has little chemical effect, but it is less beneficial than fresh organic matter in improving the physical conditions of the soil, or in stimulating activities of the beneficial soil organisms."

Degroff and Haystead, in *The Business of Farming* (University of Oklahoma Press), say:

The more there is of organic matter in the soil and the more rapid its decomposition, the more rapidly plants will grow." Note the expression "the more rapid its decomposition." There must be this dynamic movement for humus to exert its full value. It is of little use if it does not break down. Another writer refers to it as the organic balance—the balance between the constant addition and the constant subtraction of humus.

We should bear in mind that organic matter as such is much more dynamic than the humus which it produces. When you apply fresh organic matter to the land there should begin at once a strong movement of decomposition if conditions are right. Of course the rate of decay for a thin-stemmed legume plant will be much faster than for a whole corncob. This process begins as soon as the organic matter is covered with earth. If left on the soil surface, the rate of decay will be much slower. When some of the organic matter turns to humus there will be a slower rate of decay. The humus much more slowly begins to break apart so as to give some of its nutrients to the soil solution.

Nitrogen in New and Old Soils

Adrian J. Pieters, in his *Green Manuring* (John Wiley & Sons, 1927), compares humus from a new soil and from an old soil. The new soil contained 8.12 per cent nitrogen, the old, 6½ per cent. The new soil also contained much more in the way of minerals, which indicates that it is not only nitrogen that is given off in the stream from fresh humus. The fact is that the whole array of minerals is held in the organic matter and a fast decomposition releases more of it for use by plants. A great part of the soil phosphorus, for example, is held in the organic matter. In a study of *Iowa Soils* (Pearson and Simonson), it was found that between 27 and 72 per cent of the total phosphorus present was in the organic matter.

Quoting from Lyon and Buckman, *Nature and Properties of Soils* (courtesy of The Macmillan Co., copyright 1950): "In recent years, Baumann by his researches has shown freshly precipitated organic matter to possess properties which are largely colloidal in nature (very fine). Among these characteristics are high water capacity, great absorptive power for certain salts, ready mixture with other colloids, power to decompose salts, great shrinkage on drying, and coagulation in the presence of electrolytes." These characteristics would not be present, or would be present to a much lesser extent, in older humus. All of these powers are part of the formula of dynamism. It speaks of action and fast movement.

During the decay of organic matter certain acid substances are produced which have a solvent action on minerals, thus making them more soluble, and available to plants. One of the principal acids is carbonic acid. These acids are produced with the aid of micro-organisms—bacteria, fungi, et cetera. A certain amount of carbon dioxide is important to the production of crop yields. It saturates the soil water, forming an acid solution which has a solvent action on the minerals in the soil, making them available for plant use. Thus we see the main reason for keeping a fresh supply of organic matter in the soil.

In the process of humus formation when the decomposition gets to a certain point it slows down. A certain portion becomes resistant to the activities of micro-organisms and remains in an undecomposed state. There is a point then where there is a hold-up in the composition for a period of time. Under some conditions the decomposition process stops altogether and eventually peat or coal is produced. This is where the soil becomes more or less permanently covered with water, and asphyxiation occurs. If there is little addition of organic matter from year to year in a soil, after a while it will contain humus that is old and which lacks the required dynamic quality. This is what happens in farms and gardens where too much dependence is placed upon chemical fertilizers.

Aerobic and Anaerobic Conditions

In cases where anaerobic conditions exist—that is, where air is lacking—there is a slower decomposition. In considering this point there is a difference as to whether the anaerobic conditions exist in a composting process outside of the soil or whether they are in the soil itself. In an aerobic decay there is an oxidation which, roughly speaking, is a "burning out" process. If it occurs in the soil, as the nutrients stream out of the humus they are captured and held to a certain extent by the soil. But if this oxidation occurs in an ordinary compost heap, much of it dissipates itself into the atmosphere. In analyses of compost made by both processes it always holds true that the anaerobic compost has much more nitrogen and other nutrients.

In the soil, however, we want an aerobic condition. Anaerobic decomposition in composting destroys less, so that more is available for dynamic decay in the soil. But of course it is more difficult and costly to maintain anaerobic conditions in a composting process, and that is the problem. It is good to know the correct theory even though we cannot always practice it. Ideally, anaerobic conditions in compost making are the best. In the soil, conditions should be aerobic.

This was the basis of our advocating a change in the organic method a few years ago. Up to that time it was considered incorrect, according to accepted organic principles, to do other than make compost by the aerobic process. In the *Agricultural Testament,* Sir Albert Howard also recommended sheet composting, which means the application of raw organic matter to the soil. But in the fervor of practicing the method, the emphasis seemed to be mainly on composting. Rarely was a word spoken in regard to mulching. When compost is put on the land in a finished form it tends to disappear much more rapidly than when raw organic matter is applied. The latter decays much more slowly, thus releasing nutrients gradually, and as needed. Examine a piece of soil after each kind of treatment and you will see a big difference in the surface physical structure.

Taking Advantage of the Dynamic Quality of Humus

What is our attitude now? For the most part the farmer should apply most of his organic matter in a raw form to the land and permit its dynamic, moving qualities to assert themselves there. He will get the most out of it that way. The gardener will do some composting and some mulching. Occasionally he will dig in some ground-up raw organic matter, out of season.

The lesson is clear! We now understand that decomposition takes place in a soil as well as in a compost heap and that we must not be afraid to apply raw organic matter directly to the soil. We know a little more than we did before about the term "finished compost," as used by the gardener. Compost is far from a finished substance. We must learn so to choose and so to handle our organic matter that when it *is* applied to the soil it will return to us the most value.

EIGHT

CARBON-NITROGEN RATIO IN THE SOIL AND ITS IMPORTANCE

There are two chemical elements in organic matter which are extremely important, especially in their relation or proportion to each other. They are carbon and nitrogen. This relationship or proportion is called the *carbon-nitrogen ratio*. To understand what this relationship is, suppose a certain batch of organic matter is made up of 40 per cent carbon and 2 per cent nitrogen. Dividing 40 by 2, one gets 20. The carbon-nitrogen ratio of this material is then 20:1, which means twenty times as much carbon as nitrogen. Suppose another specimen has 35 per cent carbon and 5 per cent nitrogen. The carbon-nitrogen ratio of this material then would be 7:1. Anyone who handles organic matter, who mulches or composts—regardless of which method is used—should have some idea about the significance of the term carbon-nitrogen ratio. An ideal carbon-nitrogen ratio would be about 15:1.

Carbon is important because it is an energy-producing factor, nitrogen because it builds tissue.

Too much nitrogen is undesirable, because it causes many crops to go to leaf. For example, in a pepper plant one wants a certain amount of leaves, but it is the peppers that are looked for. Too much nitrogen might create a fine leaf crop but a meager amount of peppers. There is also evidence that too much carbon can bring about disease in plants. When organic matter decays, the carbon is dissipated more rapidly than the nitrogen, thus bringing down the carbon-nitrogen ratio.

Typical Carbon-Nitrogen Ratios

Before we go further and study the significance of the carbon-nitrogen ratio, let us look at some figures—examples of typical materials and their specific carbon-nitrogen ratios. Here is a list as obtained from several sources:

	C:N RATIO
Young sweet clover	12:1
Alfalfa hay	13:1
Rotted manure	20:1
Clover residues	23:1
Green rye	36:1
Sugar-cane trash	50:1
Cornstalks	60:1
Oat straw	74:1
Straw	80:1
Timothy	80:1
Sawdust	400:1

Note the high carbon-nitrogen ratio of sawdust. Such a material would be called highly carbonaceous, and it has a very low nitrogen content. If much of it is put into the soil, there will not be enough nitrogen, which is the food of bacteria and fungi that have the function of decomposing it. They would thus have to consume soil nitrogen and create a deficiency of it there, thus depressing the crop yield. The gardener who applies organic matter had best be conversant with the carbon-nitrogen ratio of the different materials he handles. Generally speaking, the legumes are highest in nitrogen and have a low carbon-nitrogen ratio, which is a highly desirable condition. The above figures are not standard, but vary greatly, depending on particular conditions under which the plants grow. Straw, for example, could go to as high as a 160:1 ratio, whereas the above gives it as 80:1.

There is a difference between the carbon-nitrogen ratio of raw organic matter and that of humus. The nitrogen in a leaf, for instance, may be only one per cent, but by the time it turns to humus, the percentage of nitrogen of that more or less refined substance would be about 5 per cent. The average of nitrogen of practically all humus is about 5 per cent, but that of organic matter fluctuates considerably. However, in regard to carbon, a different condition exists. While organic matter in decomposing loses large amounts of carbon as it turns to humus, the percentage of it to the total mass does not seem to go up or down too much. Thus, if you start with some rotted manure that has a 40 per cent carbon and 2 per cent nitrogen content, which gives a carbon-nitrogen ratio of 20:1, you may wind up with a 10:1 ratio when it turns to humus: that is, a 50 per cent carbon and a 5 per cent nitrogen content. There is always a narrowing down of the carbon-nitrogen ratio when organic matter decomposes. The content of carbon in humus does not vary too much. It averages about 50 to 52 per cent.

The carbon-nitrogen ratio of the soil is on the average much less than that of organic matter. By the time green matter is decomposed in the soil the C:N ratio has dropped to much lower figures. Waksman, in his book *Humus,* gives typical figures. Some brown silt loam soils of Illinois were about 12:1 in the topsoil, 11½:1 in the subsurface layer, and 9:1 in the subsoil. The ratio always declines as one goes downward. In the Broadbalk plots (England) the C:N ratio starts at about 9:1 and declines to about 6:1 seven feet down. Waksman cites a black clay loam at 12:1 in the topsoil and 9:1 in the subsoil. As the age of the humus increases, says Waksman, the C:N ratio of the soil in which it is becomes lower. In eight soils in northwestern United States the C:N average was 12½:1 in the top six inches, and 9:1 about three and one half feet down.

C:N Ratio of Micro-organisms

Now that we have seen that raw organic matter has a higher carbon-nitrogen ratio than humus or that of the average soil, let us look at the C:N ratio of the micro-organisms of the soil. We will find that it is usually much lower than that of organic matter, humus, or soil. The average C:N ratio of the bodies of bacteria and fungi falls between 4:1 to 10:1. Why is their C:N ratio always less than that of the humus in which they work? The answer is that they require more protein than carbohydrates. Protein is needed for tissue building mainly, while carbon of carbohydrates is for energy. Humus is made up to a great extent of lignins and other high-carbon material. In other words, humus has more carbohydrates than the bodies of microbes, which are extremely high in protein, and since about 16 per cent of protein is nitrogen, we can see that the microbes' bodies will have a very high percentage of nitrogen to carbon. Usually the tissues of bacteria are richer in protein than that of fungi.

When much raw organic matter is applied to a soil, the microorganisms will multiply rapidly, but in the process of working they have to consume nitrogen. This is absolutely necessary to their existence. Now if the material that is plowed under has a low C:N ratio—that is, low in nitrogen—the soil organisms, in decomposing it, will have to look for their nitrogen in places other than in the decomposing substances. They will draw on the soil's store of nitrogen, thus depleting it, with a depressing effect on the crop yield. But their bodies are now gorged with nitrogen, and when they die, future crops will benefit. This indicates that when plowing under highly carbonaceous organic matter a sufficient period of time should elapse before the crop is planted. It will give the soil organisms time to die, so to speak. Or one should try to use organic materials with a low C:N ratio, which means a high nitrogen content.

One investigator (Broadbalk) discovered that where the C:N ratio of added organic matter plowed under was 33:1 or more, a withdrawal of nitrogen occurred. Between 17 and 33, nothing was added or withdrawn; in other words, nitrification ceased. But if it was under 17, the nitrogen store of the soil was increased. This shows the value of adding compost to the soil, because its C:N ratio is usually quite low.

The practice is, when plowing under organic matter with a high C:N, to apply with it a high nitrogen fertilizer. For such purposes the organic gardener can use dried blood, bone meal, hen manure, cottonseed meal, fish scraps and dried ground fish, peanut shell, silk and wool wastes, castor pomace, cotton-gin wastes, cowpea and soybean hay, felt wastes, feathers, hoof or horn meal, and a number of other organic materials having a high nitrogen content.

Russell, in his book *Soil Conditions & Plant Growth* (Longmans, Green & Co.), gives an interesting illustration of a comparison between the earthworm and micro-organisms in reducing the C:N ratio of rye straw. He says, "Thus, L. Meyer found that earthworms feeding on rye straw composted with basalt meal reduced its C:N ratio from 23 to 11 during a period of two years while the soil micro-organisms alone reduced it to about 18 during the same period." This means that the earthworm is a better conserver of nitrogen than micro-organisms.

The Significance of the C:N Ratio

We have already seen that the C:N ratio of plowed-under organic matter is important to the conservation of the soil's store of nitrogen. It is also of great significance to the general operation of soils. Mainly, it is a matter of having enough nitrogen available. There is a difference in the way a low C:N ratio works, depending on whether it is in raw organic matter or in humus. In Chapter Seven we discussed the dynamic action of organic matter and showed that organic matter, applied to the soil, represents nitrogen on the move. In a finished compost it is in a more static condition—less is given off. In terms of C:N ratio, we can express it in the following manner. In the application of raw organic matter, the extent of nitrogen movement depends on its C:N ratio. If it is high, such as in sawdust (400:1), there will be no nitrogen movement; but if it is a material like young sweet clover (12:1), there will be a very satisfactory rate of nitrification.

In humus, however, although the C:N is low—let us say 10:1 —there is a resistance to rapid decomposition. The movement is slower and will take place over a longer period of time. This is of some value, as it means the nitrogen is stored for future use. In the case of fresh organic matter with a low C:N, not only is there a fast nitrogen movement but much carbon is given off in the form of carbon dioxide. It is thought by some that this may kill off some of the larvae of destructive insects.

The younger the plant material is, the lower the C:N ratio, which means that it will not only decompose more quickly but will release more nitrogen and increase the yield. Louis M.

Thompson, in his book *Soils and Soil Fertility,* gives the figures of an experiment with wheat that is typical:

STATE OF GROWTH	C:N RATIO
Very young	16
Well headed	27
Almost ripe	41

This experiment showed that the lower the C:N, the more nitrates were added to the soil and more growth of wheat occurred.

Sir Albert Howard, in *An Agricultural Experiment,* says: "In Rhodesia crops of *san* hemp are now regularly grown to provide litter, rich in nitrogen, for mixing with maize (corn) stalks so as to improve the C:N ratio of the bedding used in the cattle kraals." I cite this to show that organic farmers and even gardeners can grow special material for use in providing the best kind of organic matter for their crops, and in some cases it may be advisable to harvest these crops at an early stage in order to get a lower C:N ratio. I know of the case of a tobacco company that went into the making of compost on a large scale. They purchased large quantities of alfalfa and clover in order to get a good C:N ratio, a rapid decomposition, and a high-quality compost.

Rainfall and Temperature

As rainfall goes down, the C:N ratio also declines. The higher the rainfall, the lower the nitrogen. The C:N ratio of arid soils is always lower than those in regions of higher precipitation. It has been found that in a soil which has a rainfall of fifteen inches per annum the C:N was 13:1. Where it was ten inches or less of rain the C:N was about 11:1. It has also been found that the higher the temperature, the lower the C:N. To review: Higher rain—higher C:N. Higher temperature—lower C:N. Also: Higher acidity—higher C:N.

Waksman, in his book *Humus,* states that the carbon-nitrogen ratio of the soil humus remained almost unaffected by the addition of chemical fertilizer nitrogen. The application of organic matter high in nitrogen is necessary for the continuous accumulation of humus. No work has been done on comparative studies of the C:N ratio of organically handled soils as against chemically handled soils. Therefore I can say very little about the status and effect of the C:N ratio in an organic garden as compared to similar types of places run on the chemical basis. There is room here for future research.

NINE

HOW TO MAKE COMPOST

In the organic method we sometimes make compost, but at times we apply the organic matter in raw form to the soil. There are many methods of making compost, but the gardener will be unable to do it completely by the anaerobic method—that is, without permitting air to enter the material—because of the cost of building the equipment. Although the anaerobic method conserves more of the nitrogen, if the composter is careful, he can still turn out a product with adequate nitrogen content. He should follow a scientific plan in making compost. The old-fashioned method of throwing odds and ends of plant-matter residues promiscuously, any old which way, on a careless-looking heap is outmoded by more modern methods. In this chapter I will outline the Sir Albert Howard way of making compost, which is based on more than thirty years of experimenting and research.

Location of Heap

First choose a good site for the heap, preferably protected on the north, east, and west by a wall, fence, or hedge. Have it as close to the garden as possible, and near your supply of water, because in dry weather you will have to water it every day. Pick out a flat location that is well drained, and one that is not near the bottom of a hill, where the rains will come shooting down. Reserve a place next to the heap where you can pile your green waste materials such as weeds, grass clippings, et cetera, for it is best to let such material wither a while before being placed in the compost heap. You do not want too much sun or too much wind. The latter will stop fermentation.

Size of Heap

The size will depend on the area of your garden and on the amount of material you have available for composting, but the minimum should be about six feet square. The height, regardless of the square area, should be five feet. The maximum width in the case of large heaps should be about twelve feet, otherwise air will not be able to penetrate the inside. The length can be almost any size. In India, Sir Albert Howard has stated, heaps have been made more than thirty or forty feet long. The height, however, remains at five feet. A good size for the average small garden would be about five feet wide by twelve feet long. I have seen much excellent compost made, however, in which the heaps were only four feet high.

Materials Used in Heap

It is best to accumulate a reserve of green waste materials for future use. This may consist of leaves, weeds, grass clippings, cornstalks, sunflower stalks, hedge trimmings, seaweed, spoiled hay and straw, kitchen wastes, chaff, and any other kind of plant material you can find. In many cases you will find neighboring land growing wild in weeds. You can always get permission to cut them down. By doing so, you not only obtain material for composting, but if you cut the weeds down before they go to seed, you prevent the seeds from blowing over your land.

There are many by-products and materials in the industrial life of cities and towns which yield valuable organic matter for composting. In the fish department of the average vegetable market there is a great accumulation of fish cuttings, entrails, heads, et cetera, which is given away for the asking. This may be used as a manure substitute in the compost heap. Breweries give away what is called brewery waste, which consists of the hulls of grains used in making liquors, after the inside of the grains has been pressed out. This is valuable plant material. In the vegetable department at groceries and at wholesale establishments large quantities of the green tops of vegetables accumulate. In your own house are the table cuttings and even the vacuum-cleaner dust. The fish heads, meat scraps, and eggshells contain valuable nutritional ingredients. Even barbershop hair residues can be used—they are extremely rich in nitrogen. Sawdust sweepings from butcher shops, fish-shop wastes, straw, sewage sludge, silk mill wastes, coffee grounds from restaurants, wool wastes, ground bark, cannery wastes, sugarcane wastes in the South, tobacco factory residues, spoiled milk, nutshells, oyster shells, horse manure, citrus wastes, cotton-gin wastes, and feathers are only a few examples of what is available to the eager organic gardener.

In chicken markets much organic material is thrown out or sent to be burned at the city incinerator, consisting of the entrails, head, feet, and feathers of chickens, cage scrapings, sawdust—all of which is available as a substitute for, if not an improvement upon, manure. Near our farm, which is only about ninety-five miles from New York City, a considerable amount of trapping of small animals is carried on in the winter. After the skins are taken off, the rest of the carcasses are dumped somewhere. While it is unwise to use these on the land in their raw state, they are very valuable material if composted. An enterprising person will find much other material available if he keeps his eyes open.

GRINDING LEAVES   Using decayed leaves as a fertilizer in a garden is an age-old device. Leaves are one of the finest fertilizer materials available, because tree roots go down to depths of twenty-five feet or more and feed to the leaves the inexhausted minerals found at those levels. In the U. S. Department of Agriculture 1938 Yearbook, *Soils and Men*, it is stated on page 516, "Leaves alone, when dry, are about twice as rich per pound in plant food as barnyard manure." It is known from experience that remarkable results are produced in gardening with leaf mold. The leaf is a factory, a crucible in which all the nutritive elements work to make fruit, blossoms, seed, et cetera. It is an extremely rich substance for use in making compost.

Ordinarily we do not advise the use of leaves exclusively in making a compost heap. Of the six inches of green matter required in the layer, we advise a small amount of leaves. If leaves were used entirely, it would tend to pack and prevent aeration. However, this would not be true of ground leaves. They could be used in the entire layer.

By the old method it takes a year or two to turn a heap of leaves into leaf mold. By the Sir Albert Howard process it can be done in three or four months. Through accident I discovered a method by which leaves can be used immediately without composting. This discovery came about in a peculiar manner.

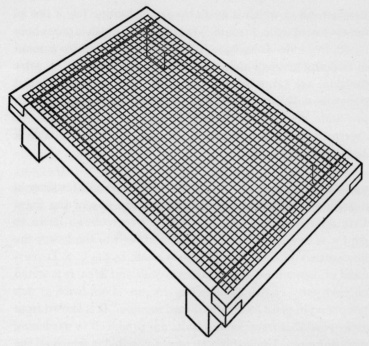

½″ HARDWARE CLOTH SCREEN

I had taken an old book from my bookshelves and was going over it when a page fell out. In handling it, it began to crumble. I carefully replaced the page and put the book back on the shelf. That evening, while seated at the supper table, I saw the leaves falling outside, floating slowly downward in all their beautiful colors. Suddenly I remembered the old page of the book that had crumbled and quickly went to the shelves and removed it. Without thinking of the value of the book, I took that sheet and crumbled it to bits with my hands. It had become so dry and crisp with age that it was broken into a thousand tiny fragments. I could hardly wait until next morning to gather some leaves and see how quickly they could be dried.

I placed them under cover, and within a few days was able to crumble them into a powder. It is surprising how easy it is to crumble goodly quantities of leaves with the hands without the aid of any equipment whatever. By wearing gloves greater pressure can be applied. If, however, your requirements are too great, you can use hand-worked screens to expedite the process.

Make a screen in a frame approximately two by three feet, using half-inch screen wire sold in any hardware store. Its trade name is hardware cloth, half-inch size. It is simple to force the leaves through these screen meshes with your hands. You then screen this product through your second frame, which is made

¼″ HARDWARE CLOTH SCREEN

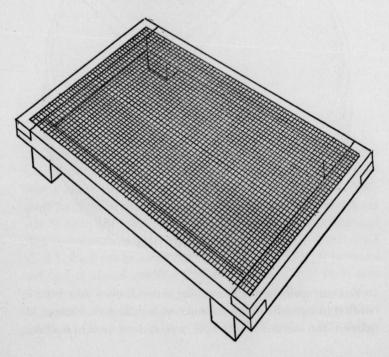

with a quarter-inch-size screen, so that the product comes out a little finer. If you find it more difficult to procure the eighth-inch screening for the last frame, a household flour sieve can be used. You can make a fourth screen out of mosquito-wire screening if you want the product to be extra fine. It is suggested that gloves be worn for ease of working the material through. There are variations of this equipment which the intelligent gardener can improvise to suit his own situation, and the equipment is most inexpensive.

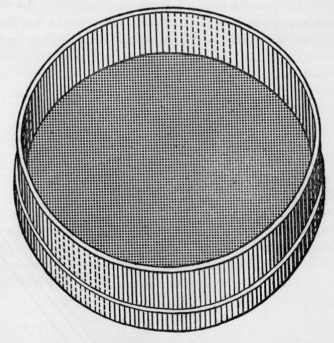

BAKERS FLOUR SIEVE

You can sprinkle this ground-up material over your lawn or work it in immediately in the top few inches of your vegetable garden. You can mix it with sand, soil, and compost in seed flats and let it season in your cellar during the winter for starting your vegetable seedlings next spring. It can be worked into flower and shrubbery beds. It can also be stored in the cellar all winter, mixed with a little topsoil, and watered regularly to turn into finished compost by spring. If ground fine in a coffee grinder, it can be used for flowerpot plants. If coarser, it can be used for a mulch in a flowerpot. It makes an ideal food for earthworms, as the worms are extremely fond of leaves and consume this finely ground-up material in a short time.

In this process the stems do not become pulverized but will disintegrate rapidly in the soil. However, they should be picked out if the material is to be used in flowerpots.

From experience and observation it is known that the smaller the piece of green matter, the quicker it will decay. If you use whole cornstalks in the compost heap, they may not decay in the three-month period, but if you chop them up, they will decompose rapidly. Smaller leaf plants, such as clover, will decay faster than large, coarse-leaved weeds, and the further reduction in size by grinding will hasten the decay. A small piece becomes more saturated with moisture. Air can get at it more easily. On the other hand, there is a point beyond which the reduction in size would become detrimental in the decay processes. For example, sawdust in small quantities will decompose in a compost heap, whereas wood flour, which represents wood ground to the fineness of flour, will cake up and prevent aeration. I tried it as a mulch on a flower bed once and it caked up as though it were cement.

How to Make the Heap

Start off by placing a layer of plant matter about six inches high on the ground, to the width and length of your heap. Then follow it with a layer, about two inches thick, of either manure or some substance like kitchen waste. In the case of more concentrated materials, such as chicken cuttings or other meat products, the layer should be only one inch thick. Next apply a light sprinkling of lime (ground limestone) or wood ashes. Be sure that it is agricultural lime and not the stronger lime, which is referred to as gypsum, or hydrated. The lime is needed to sweeten the pile, to alkalize it, and to hasten decay. Then apply a mere sprinkling, not over one eighth of an inch, of earth, preferably rich earth full of bacteria.

Then you start the process all over again, placing six inches of green material on top of the last layer of earth, then two inches of manure, lime, and earth. You keep on until the heap reaches a height of five feet. Do not tamp it down as you make it, but leave it soft and fluffy so that the air can get into the center of the heap. Keep watering it from time to time, so that when it is finished it is damp but not too soggy. The right amount of moisture is very important. It should have about as much water as a moist sponge.

Build your heap with a taper—that is, if it is about six feet wide at the bottom, it should be about three and one half to four feet at the top—scooping out part of the top, saucer fashion, so that it will not let the rain water escape. The last layer of earth should also be much heavier and should cover the sides as well as the top. The more of a taper you give sides, the easier it will be to apply this enclosing earth. Watering is a matter of personal observation and common sense. Be sure you don't let the heap dry out. Applying a heavy straw mulch to the top and sides has been found to be very effective. It permits hosing without causing the composting material to fall apart. Also it protects it from the sun and encourages earthworms to work under it.

Make large holes about five or six inches in diameter in the compost heap as soon as it is constructed, using a crowbar or some other method. These should go from the top to the ground and should be spaced about three feet apart. They aid the aeration of the heap. Some people use pipes which are placed in position as the heap is made. These, when removed, leave well-made, roomy holes. A block of wood or some other means can be used.

Turning the Compost

The first turn takes place three weeks after the heap is made. A thorough job must be done, so that the material becomes well mixed, and an attempt should be made to see that what was on the inside gets to the outside and vice versa. This allows every part of the material to get to the place where the bacteria and the fungi are most active.

The next turn takes place five weeks after the first one, a thorough mixing being required. A five-pronged fork is best for this work. The time needed for completion varies. In India, Sir Albert Howard made compost in a three-month period. In the United States it varies depending upon locality. I would say that in this country it would vary from three to five months, depending on warmth, rain, et cetera. In the South the decomposition works more rapidly than in the North if there is sufficient water.

After completion, the compost should be applied to the soil at once. However, if this cannot be done, it should be turned from time to time—about once every two or three weeks.

Accelerating the Composting Time

One of the best ways to accelerate the composting time and to turn out a more finished compost is to sprinkle old compost into the new heap as it is being constructed. This should be done about every seven or eight inches—a bare sprinkling, that is, about an average of a quarter of an inch, merely to act as a bacterial activator. Sprinkling plenty of water each time the old compost is applied will cause the bacteria to wash down into the raw organic matter and begin the processes of decay sooner. In controlled experiments which we have made with and without old compost activators, it is remarkable how much better the compost is by the former method which can be seen with the eye and felt with the hand. There can be no question about it, yet the average gardener overlooks this little help which can be such a great aid to better gardening. There are commercial bacterial activators on the market which may be used for the same purpose. A solution may be made by soaking manure in water and using the water part only as the activator. A diluted solution of urine is also an excellent activator.

TEN

MISCELLANEOUS METHODS OF COMPOSTING

Composting of plant and animal residues has been a device resorted to by the gardener from time immemorial. But it was not until Sir Albert Howard explored the behavior of organic matter while undergoing decomposition that a beginning was made in the development of a science. Sir Albert demonstrated some striking principles which have been explained in a previous chapter, but his mind was not rigidly closed to any further expansion or growth in this age-old art. I have already stated that compost making is an art, also a science—it partakes of both—it is to a certain extent adaptable to the needs, the experience, the realities, and the preferences of the compost maker. In organic gardening the fertility of the soil increases so startlingly that sometimes convenience dictates the employment of a method that gives less nutrients but is more adaptable to the needs or preferences of a particular gardener.

The Earthworm Method

In the orthodox method of making compost there are two main disadvantages. One: because of the earth bottom, much valuable liquid containing large amounts of valuable nutrients leaches out from below. Two: because the materials are piled five feet high, a strong heat decomposition takes place. Such oxidation destroys nutrients, bacteria, and valuable enzymes. In watching earthworms breeding in our earthworm boxes, I saw that they were turning out a compost of the highest quality. In these boxes the materials are never more than two feet high, and I have never noticed any heating in them. One of the factors preventing this is that we thoroughly mix the various raw organic materials which go into these earthworm boxes. Secondly, the earthworms immediately penetrate into the matter, working it up thoroughly. So there seem to be three factors to prevent heating in the way these boxes are constituted:

1. The raw material is not more than two feet high.
2. There is thorough mixing of the raw materials.
3. The earthworm acts as the decomposing agent.

In this method the compost can be made in boxes indoors or in pits on the outside. The boxes should not be more than two feet high, but their width and length are optional. The same applies to the construction of a pit. It can be of any width or length that is convenient; it can be of any shape—square, oblong, or even round. As earthworms do not like light, it is desirable to make a wooden top, one that is not too tight-fitting. When it rains the cover should be removed, for rain water is of great value as a watering agent.

A variety of materials are placed in the pit and thoroughly mixed. The more they are mixed, the less tendency there is to heat up. See that the mass is well watered and put the earthworms in immediately. These should be of the domestic variety advertised for sale in *Organic Gardening*. The more earthworms that are put in, the quicker the composting will take place. In a pit ten feet square it would be nothing to put in ten thousand earthworms. They breed very fast if you start breeding them indoors. This method itself is practically a method of breeding earthworms which can be used for various purposes, such as feeding to chickens or placing in a mass of raw organic matter used as a mulch. One need not purchase more than a thousand or two earthworms, as they will multiply fantastically. Full instructions as to how to breed and feed them are usually given by the earthworm breeder.

The action of the earthworms will produce the finest compost you can ever make. Their castings will thoroughly impregnate the mass with a material extremely rich in all the nutrients and trace-mineral elements. It will become darker than compost made by other methods. As soon as the material is assembled and the earthworms placed in it, cover the entire top of the pit with rocks or old boards. Conditions of darkness will make the earthworms work better and the composting time will be greatly reduced. The rocks or boards will also conserve moisture. If the top is not covered, the time element will be increased. Try to find flat stones that would be light to handle. The thinner type of purchased flagstones would be excellent for this purpose. By this method compost can be made in two months or less.

Such a pit is an excellent place for the family garbage. Coffee grounds are excellent feed for earthworms. They seem to thrive on them. To enable the earthworms to make a better compost, buy some ground whole wheat and mix it in with the materials. You can use other seeds, ground up, such as soybeans, corn, et cetera. The ordinary garden angleworm cannot be used in this box method as it does not thrive or work under these conditions.

Earthworm Green-Matter Formula

In the boxes a typical mixture would be about 70 per cent weeds, leaves, grass clippings, et cetera, about 15 per cent manure and 15 per cent topsoil. This can be greatly varied. If no manure is available, parts of your table wastes can be substituted. You can try almost any formula.

One subject which never has been thoroughly studied is that of the enzymes in the composting process. Since enzymes are destroyed at 40° centigrade (104° Fahrenheit), and since compost heaps get up to about 160° Fahrenheit, it would appear that all of the enzymes are destroyed. But in the earthworm boxes the heat would not reach such danger points.

We must also be aware that manures and green matter contain vitamins. One rarely sees mention of this. We are told that in cooking foods much of the vitamin content is destroyed by heat. Therefore, why should this not also be true of vitamins in a compost heap?

Do not put too much water in the boxes or it will create an anaerobic condition, which will impede the earthworms from working properly.

The process takes about sixty days. Then you take out half a box of material and fill it up with the raw materials again. In sixty days the new stuff will be completely composted. It is advisable to feed the earthworms something equivalent to chicken mash, but you can make your own feed, using ground leaves and ground grain seeds such as wheat, barley, corn. This food is sprinkled lightly on top. I have noticed that in the pits where we placed the earthworms less weeds grew on top, which leads me to believe that these little fellows chew up the weed seeds along with the other materials and take the sting out of them. This is terrifically important if true. When the compost is taken out of the pit we leave some of it at the bottom to act as an inoculant for the new material. The earthworms it contains will enter the new heap as soon as the heating has ceased.

The Lehigh Compost Box Method

Many gardeners prefer to make compost in pits, wooden boxes, and so forth. Some have used wooden barrels, steel drums, and many other ingenious devices. Here is a method

LEHIGH COMPOST BOX

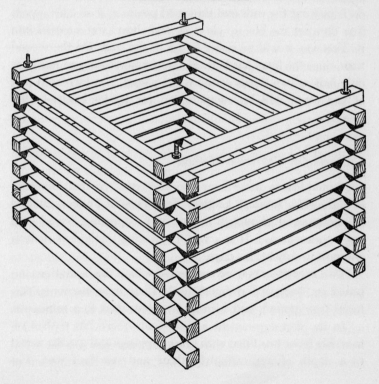

I worked out—a type of bin which any person can assemble without tools of any kind. The picture gives you the idea. There is not a single nail in the whole thing. You can make it of a size to suit your needs. It is made of two-by-fours, or heavier lumber if your purse can stand it. Ask the lumberyard to drill three-quarter-inch holes near each end, unless you are handy and have the tools yourself. Then secure round iron rods, one half inch in diameter, and force them into the ground for about six inches to give rigidity to the bin. The picture will illustrate what I mean.

Such rods are sold in the bigger hardware stores or mill supply concerns. If you want to turn the heap, all you have to do is pull out the rods and the wood pieces will all come apart. You then set the box up close by and shovel the material into it. This way it will be easier to get at the stuff. On the second turn, since the heap has become more compacted, you need use only half or two thirds of the wood pieces. The increased cost of the wood will be compensated for by its longer-lasting qualities.

University of California Method

I would like to quote from a booklet issued by the University of California, Sanitary Engineering Research Project, entitled *Reclamation of Municipal Refuse by Composting*, issued June 1953 (price $1.00). It is a very interesting method of making compost in only twelve days.

"Two experiments were conducted within the limitations imposed by 'Backyard' composting. In these experiments no material was ground, and turning was restricted to a minimum.

"In the first experiment a three-foot-square bin with a removable front was filled with grass clippings and garden weeds to a depth of approximately three and one half feet. The material was turned every other day. Temperature rise and fall followed a normal course.

"Composting was completed within twelve days and an excellent product rich in nitrogen, phosphorus, and potassium resulted.

"The second experiment involved the use of a wider variety of materials. Grass clippings, entire dahlia plants, whole heads of lettuce and cauliflower, dry garden weeds, dry sycamore leaves, avocado seeds, and some kitchen refuse, were placed in a bin without shredding in any manner. Because of the dry leaves and weeds, the mass was sprinkled at the start to increase the moisture content. The material was turned every other day. The sycamore leaves were slow to break down. However, within thirteen days, the process was complete and a very satisfactory product resulted. No initial analysis was made because of the difficulty in obtaining a representative sample.

"These experiments show that even in a fairly small volume, material ordinarily encountered in gardens and in kitchen wastes, excluding paper and large bones, can be composted readily and rapidly without preliminary grinding or any treatment other than turning every other day."

Finished Compost in Fourteen Days

Shredding of all material before it goes into the compost heap is the key to fast composting. We proved that with experiments at our organic gardening experimental farm and in our own home gardens. Frequent turning—as often as every three days—is also important. Shredded compost is very easy to turn. It offers little resistance to your shovel, and a one-ton heap can be turned in five to ten minutes.

In order to present to readers an accurate picture of fast composting methods, we got together the three garden-size compost shredders that are now being marketed. They were the Kemp Model 6, the Keston Shredder, and the W–W model 2–XB. The Kemp and the W–W shredders were equipped with 2–hp gasoline engines and the Keston with an electric motor.

The first shredder to arrive was the Kemp Model 6. We took it to our own back yard, along with two bales of spoiled hay, two drums of dry corncobs, and a drum of horse manure. We also used a few shovelfuls of finished compost for a starter. First we began putting through the machine several bushels of iris that a friend had contributed. They were mashed up admirably, but the stringy stalks stalled the engine if they were fed too fast. We found that feeding a corncob with each large handful of iris cleared the machine nicely.

The cobs themselves were shredded all right, but they made a lot of noise inside the machine. That started us feeding some hay with the cobs, in order to cushion them. Finally we ran through the hay and manure. Both were shredded into quite small particles. All in all, we were quite impressed, because the Kemp (and the W–W) is primarily intended as a grinder of finished compost and soil. It worked well for our purpose, however. We expected fast developments but were quite surprised next morning to see the temperature up to 130 degrees. Even more interesting was the color, which had changed overnight from a light yellow to a light brown.

Monday evening we turned it for the first time, noting that the color was even darker and the heat greater. A ring of white, air-loving fungus had begun to grow around the edges of the heap. According to scientists, the area around the edges of a compost heap breaks down first, because of the action of these fungi. The strongest decay-causing organisms need plenty of air. That is why the heap should be turned often.

The following Saturday—one week after the heap was made— it was turned for the second time. The ring mold was very noticeable. From a distance of a few feet, the heap looked finished already. But on closer inspection you could see that it needed some time to simmer down. Ten days after the heap was made it was quite dark brown in color and soft to the touch. We judged the heap finished and ready for use. It had not stopped heating entirely, but it certainly looked like finished compost, and its nutrients were in a readily available state. We had succeeded in making compost in two weeks, using easily obtained materials.

We also field-tested the Keston and the W–W shredders. The Keston is a knife shredder. It consists of a revolving drum on which is mounted a series of triangular mower blades. These rotating blades pass near a set of stationary blades. The Keston machine handled spoiled hay, garbage, cornstalks, and tall weeds. It looks as though it would do a good job on leaves, but because of the season we didn't have any to try. The Keston does the fastest job of shredding, but does not break material down as finely as the Kemp or the W–W. That is not a serious fault, however.

The W–W grinder, like the Kemp, is intended primarily as a grinder of finished compost and soil. But the ability of both shredders to handle fresh material is not greatly sacrificed. The W–W is a hammer mill, and the user has the choice of two screen sizes, one for compost and one for fresh material. We used the W–W on a mixture of tough green weeds and it did a good job. It could certainly handle leaves, garbage, and other compost raw materials.

One thing you shouldn't overlook when thinking about compost grinders is that they do a good job of making mulch material. Spoiled hay, for example, doesn't make an attractive mulch for flower beds, but if it is run through a shredder, it becomes an attractive and easy-to-handle mulch. A shredded mulch keeps down weeds better too.

Here is our summary of the three machines tested:

KEMP. Produces a fine consistency of shredded material and is safe and easy to feed. Not so easy to move as the other two machines. Can be stalled by feeding stringy material too fast, but is easy to clear and start again.

KESTON. Is very portable and is least expensive of the three machines. Does a good job on most fresh organic matter.

W–W. Shreds fresh compost material well and is quite portable. Ejects tough material in separate pile at end of machine. Can also be stalled by fresh stringy material, but is easily cleared.

The Anaerobic Method of Making Compost

Organic Gardening magazine made its bow in June 1942, introducing a new concept of soil fertility. Its teachings were readily accepted, and things were moving along serenely until about December 1949, when it numbered about one hundred thousand readers. At that time a little storm was stirred up by the writer of this book, and here is how it came about. In the summer of 1949 the Soil and Health Foundation, of which I am president, hired Dr. Charles Selvi of Italy to work in the laboratory located on our experimental farm. Up until this time the idea of making compost under aerobic conditions (having access to air) had become so well established that any change was considered downright heresy. But Dr. Selvi had accomplished research in Italy which indicated that aerobic composting was a "burning up" of some of the nutrients in the materials undergoing reduction. When he saw organic matter being composted in open pits and heaps, he threw up his hands in horror. Dr. Selvi had been an Italian Government agronomist who had studied fermentation. He drew my attention to the weaknesses of the aerobic method (using air). During heavy rains much of the nutrient matter leached out from below. The high heat of the aerobic fermentation (about 160 degrees F.) combusted out much of the nutrient matter, sending it into the air. Selvi had found in Italy that whereas manure kept in open pits lost 40 per cent of the nitrogen originally contained, manure in a closed pit lost only from 2 to 10 per cent of nitrogen, depending on how tight the pit was closed and how much it was opened for inspection.

Research has proven conclusively that an anaerobic fermentation preserves more of the nutrients. Professor Selman A. Waksman and Florence G. Tenny, of the New Jersey Agricultural Experiment Station, did some research comparing the aerobic and anaerobic decomposition of various types of organic matter which was recorded in *Soil Science* of August 1930. In it the authors say, "In a study made on the decomposition of immature oak leaves under aerobic and anaerobic conditions, it was shown that when the leaf material was saturated with water, the celluloses and hemicelluloses were decomposed much more slowly than when the material was under aerobic conditions; the fats and waxes were much more resistant to decomposition and the lignins were preserved almost quantitatively, whereas the protein content of anaerobic material was considerably greater than that of the aerobic compost because of the greater decomposition of the proteins and losses of the nitrogen in the form of ammonia in the aerobic compost."

The fact that the anaerobic storing of manure may be desirable is brought out in a recent book issued by the Food and Agriculture Organization of the United Nations entitled *The Efficient Use of Fertilizers*. It contains the following statement: "In Norway, where cattle are stall-fed throughout the winter, the manure is dropped during the daily cleaning through a trap door into a basement extending the length of the cowshed. In this manner it is well protected until used in the spring."

Further on it comments about this method as follows: "Under the efficient methods of storage described above, which are largely anaerobic [free of air], the rate of decomposition of organic matter is slow and the volatilization of ammonia reduced to a minimum. On the other hand, in dry, well-aerated manure piles there is much loss of organic matter and ammonia."

Here is an example from a more popular source, a quotation from the book *Dahlias, What Is Known About Them,* by Morgan T. Riley (Orange Judd Publishing Company, 1947): "We keep the sides of the compost heap straight, we keep the top covered with earth, we keep its top concave so that rain and water which we shall play upon it will not run off but lodge there and make the action of the bacteria anaerobic, out of the air, thus lessening loss of nitrogen."

In the study of the question of aerobic conditions against anaerobic, we must bear in mind that there is one place where conditions *must* be aerobic and that is in the soil itself.

In cases where land becomes waterlogged due to standing water and the anaerobic organisms take over, crops will suffer. But good compost *can* be made by the anaerobic method, and when it is applied to a well-aerated soil the aerobic organisms will prevail and begin to work on it to good advantage as far as crop yields and health of plant are concerned.

In Italy, Selvi was called into a certain district where tourists complained of the manure odors given off by the open pits. He designed enclosures for them and was surprised at the better crops and higher yields that such fertilizers caused. On our farm we made compost from manure under Selvi's method. Incidentally, under this system, when making compost in a pit, it is necessary to have a small drainage pit so that excess moisture can go out from the main pit. The basis of the Selvi process is that there must not be a waterlogging of the material but yet there must be enough moisture. The compost that resulted from the manure in the Selvi pit was better than that from the control pit which was open to the air.

We still make compost by the aerobic method, but we have gone in a great deal for mulching, or covering the soil with a layer of the raw organic materials. Since it is expensive to build an enclosed pit for the making of anaerobic compost, it is better to allow the green matter residues to compost in a layer of varying thickness at the spot where their resulting humus will go into the ground. When it rains, the juices will descend into the soil with the rain water rather than be washed away. There are other advantages of mulching which will be discussed in a later chapter, and we highly recommend this practice. When you consider the theory discussed in Chapter Eight, showing the advantage of having live humus in the soil—that is, organic matter with a dynamic quality, humus on the move, so to speak, which gives off a steady stream of nitrogen—then mulching is a highly desirable gardening technique.

One thing must not be overlooked. An organic garden is much richer in soil organisms, such as bacteria and fungi as well as earthworms, than a chemicalized garden. It has, therefore, a greater digestive power. These members of the biologic world of the soil are its intestines, so to speak. They can easily handle a dug-in mulch at the end of a season, and by the following spring will almost have completely digested it.

It would appear to me that so far as the requirements of the gardener are concerned, he needs only to stick to the aerobic method, making his heaps in the open, because actually his resulting fertilizer, even with the losses incurred in compost-making, will be more than adequate to satisfy the needs of the soil and plants.

IS TOO MUCH COMPOST HARMFUL?

Thus far practically nothing can be found in the literature of organic gardening which throws light on the question of a possible overuse of organic matter. Very few, if any, have given much thought to the possible dangers inherent in overstocking the soil with humus. It is a common belief that we should pile organic matter into our gardens until the earth turns black, and it is the unquenchable ambition of every organiculturist not to rest until that color is attained. But I wonder if this is desirable! Are we overdoing a good thing and are we plaguing ourselves with unnecessary work?

I recently received a sample of the soil of the Hunza country in India, sent to me by their mir, or ruler. You may be familiar with my book *The Healthy Hunzas,* which shows that the Hunzukuts are an extremely healthy people because they are very conscientious farmers, realizing that their well-being is related directly to soil fertility. I was expecting a dark soil but was greatly surprised to see a greenish tinge to it. It had a powdery aspect, giving it a feeling of finely crumbled rock. Looking at it, you would imagine that it contained no organic matter whatever. We do know that organic matter is scarce in Hunza. Yet there is a sufficient quantity in the soil to give the Hunzukuts wonderful health, because of the quality of food it produces. A good soil today must contain a considerable portion of minute rock particles to make it a proper medium for growing plants and to give it the necessary mineral content. Organic matter contains some minerals but it is also a source of vitaminlike substances of which rock is completely void. Rocks are the main mineral suppliers. To be good, a soil must contain some organic matter, but its physical structure and lack of mineral elements in the rock may militate against producing good crops.

Dr. Ehrenfried Pfeiffer attempted to determine the maximum amount of compost that would be effective in giving the optimum yield on a crop such as peas. He set up an experiment a few years ago, using varying amounts of compost in order to determine whether the use of more would create greater yields. The results indicated that in peas there was an increase in yield up to the use of five tons per acre of compost, but beyond that it remained the same. For a gardener, five tons per acre is an extremely small amount—about one pound for every four and one half square feet.

Radish Experiments

In the early days of the organic method I decided to find out how the use of extremely large quantities of compost would affect the growing of radishes. Therefore I set up three little plots. In number one no compost was added. In number two a liberal amount was put in, and in number three we dug in an amount equivalent to 100 per cent compost. Number two, with its reasonable amount of compost, gave the best radishes, from both the standpoints of size and quality of structure. In the all-compost radishes the insides were coarse-looking.

Let us look at Nature and the way in which she handles her organic matter. In many forests there is a comparatively thick growth of huge trees, but the organic matter of their soil comes from a thin annual layer of fallen leaves. Surely this is a much smaller amount of fertilizer than the average organic practitioner places in his soil. Yet the trees thrive. Think of the gigantic sequoia of California—their size, health, and age. They live off that small amount of fallen leaves, which turns to leaf mold. Of course there is some subtle alchemy that goes on in the soil because of its natural condition, and because of the presence of certain bacteria and other organisms which extract diverse things from the air and make that little go a long way. It used to be thought that the soil organisms get only nitrogen from the air. There is now evidence that they also do the same thing in regard to phosphorus. Who knows? Before all the results are in, it may be discovered that soil bacteria extract even trace minerals from the atmosphere.

Chandler, at Cornell University, in a series of studies, found that mixed hardwood trees on a Lordstown silt-loam soil produced annually one and one fourth tons of dry-leaf material per acre. On other soils (Ontario silt loam) it was one and one half tons. In France the figure for beech trees was one and one half tons of organic matter to the acre annually. In a crop of oats amounting to about forty bushels to the acre, the dry matter in the grain and straw was about the same amount. These are reasonable amounts. But some gardeners put into their soils the equivalent of one hundred tons to the acre per annum.

In the field, also, Nature is not too liberal in giving sustenance. Frugality seems to be her watchword. Here organic matter is doled out sparingly. In the tropics, however, where the humus burns out more rapidly, the growth of plants is lush and more abundant, so that its decay furnishes more humus than in more temperate climates. It is amazing how, in Nature, the requirement for sustenance thus automatically adjusts itself. When a tree is young, and its food requirements little, there is a small amount of leaf fall. As it grows and its requirements increase, the leaf fall goes up accordingly. Is there something we can learn from this?

Of course we have the problem of getting a "yield," but if the necessary research could be done, we might find, like Pfeiffer did, that the amount of organic matter required to obtain an optimum crop is nowhere near what present thinking imagines it is.

Leafage vs. Fruit

One of the dangers of using too much organic matter is that in many crops there would be too much development of leaf because of the nitrogen in the humus. The latter seems to be a good provider of nitrogen, and this element is very effective in producing vegetative growth. I distinctly remember a small apple tree to which we gave so much compost that a visiting agricultural professor, seeing it, remarked, "What wonderful leaves!" They were the thickest he had ever seen. But he wasn't there a few months later to observe the poor fruit that formed. Too much of the sustenance had gone to the leaves.

I wrote to Stark Bros. Nurseries, famous growers of fruit trees in Louisiana, Missouri, asking their opinion of the effect of too much nitrogen. They replied, "In our experience the most obvious results from the use of an excess of nitrogen on apple trees are later maturity and less red color in the skin. In the case of late fall and winter apples, there is a reduction in the sugar in the fruit and some varieties never develop a satisfactory flavor."

Dr. Selman A. Waksman, the recent Nobel prize winner and a world authority on humus, says in his book *Humus:* "Too much organic matter, especially from legumes (high in nitrogen), may not be very desirable, because it favors excessive vegetative growth of the trees."

Flower gardeners may also have noticed that bulbs and some root crops may be damaged in soils too high in organic matter content. There are some flowers that do not do well on too much compost. Here, for example, is a list of flowers which Mandeville and King suggest require a poor soil: alyssum, bachelor's-button, calliopsis, candytuft, celosia, clarkia, cosmos, four-o'clock, godetia, kochia, nasturtium, California poppy, Shirley poppy, portulaca, and verbena. Alyssum, candytuft, nasturtium, and California poppy especially give best results if grown in a poor soil.

Is it possible, also, that too much compost produces over-succulence which entices the insect? There is some evidence that overcomposting may be one of the agents in drawing insects. We saw it in our own experience with the Mexican bean beetle. This is one insect that we do not seem to be able to control in our gardens. One year, however, when we grew beans on some new ground that had received compost for the first time, the beans were far less infested with the Mexican beetle than a batch of beans growing on a soil not far away which had received compost every year for about ten years. That experience first led me to consider whether there wasn't some harm in overdoing composting.

Insects and Lushness

The insect is not here by accident. It is part of Nature's

scheme to keep things in order. She used the insect to destroy unwanted vegetation. If a growing plant is unbalanced in its nutritional content by reason of artificial methods of fertilization, if it is grown on the wrong kind of soil, as potatoes on clay with little organic matter, if an acid-loving plant is growing on an alkaline soil, if it becomes sick for any reason at all, the insects will come to attempt to destroy it. Then there is war. It is man with his spray guns against the winged enemy. There is much evidence of this role of the insect, and it is reflected in writings about the organic method. A bug, with a few exceptions, rarely comes to attack a healthy plant which is growing under the proper conditions and in the right place.

Now, if a plant is growing on a soil which has been overcomposted, it may become a candidate, from Nature's point of view, for a visit from her tiny winged policemen. There might be something about such a plant which is not quite right. Perhaps it is an oversupply of nitrogen.

We receive letters from time to time from readers who complain that although they do everything we tell them to, they still have some trouble with their vegetables. This type of letter does not come too often, but it baffles me. A gardener writes that his tomato vines produce only small tomatoes, or none at all. Could it be due to an overcomposting, the excess of nitrogen going all to leaf, leaving little for the fruit itself?

I recall reading in one of Alexis Carrel's books that a plant which grows too fast is not a healthy plant. He states that a slow, steady growth makes for the best conditions of health. We know that on the average those people who eat frugally live the longest. There is the classical case of Luigi Cornaro, who lived in Italy in the fifteen hundreds, and who was given up by his physician in his forties, because of poor health. He worked out a diet so small in quantity that it seemed almost starvation. But he lived to be close to one hundred. Medical literature is replete with experiments which prove that animals on diets of less food have less cancer. In Europe the austerity conditions and food shortages brought about by the war showed up very favorably in the mortality and health statistics. There was less disease. Today, with all their food difficulties and starvation diets, the English have a longer life span than we do. Statistics kept by the life-insurance companies show unquestionably that obesity, which is due to overconsumption of food, causes earlier deaths. Should we consider a plant growing in an overcomposted soil which shows an excellent growth and size as obese rather than succulent?

Dr. J. K. Wilson's Work with Nitrogen

There is some proof that too much nitrogen may be a hazard to health, and since humus is the principal agent that furnishes nitrogen in the soil, we have another worry now to consider. The late Dr. J. K. Wilson of Cornell wrote in the January 1949 issue of the *Agronomy Journal* that nitrites could cause poisoning through combination with the blood. He shows that possibly in rural regions nitrates from fertilizer seep into wells and cause a disease in babies drinking such water. This disease is called methemoglobinemia, or blue-baby disease. In 1947 in Illinois alone there were thirty-three cases, with five deaths. Dr. Wilson found that there was danger from the overconsumption of leafy plants which may contain too much nitrite and recommended that the following should not be overconsumed: broccoli, cabbage, cauliflower, and rhubarb. In other words, if our soil is overcharged with nitrogen through applying too much compost, there might be a danger of our leafy vegetables taking up too much of it. Dr. Wilson sums up the subject as follows: "Leafy vegetables, frozen foods, and prepared baby foods were analyzed for their content of nitrate. From the findings it is suggested that the nitrate in such foods may contribute to hemoglobinemia found in infants and may produce certain toxic, if not lethal, conditions in adults. The high content of nitrate in the foods may be attributed in many instances to the application of nitrogenous fertilizers, especially nitrate of soda, to the growing crops."

The point brought up by Dr. Wilson may not apply to organically produced vegetables, but can we be certain of it without thorough research into the subject? According to his article, it is a question of the stability of the nitrogen compound. In the form of nitrates, the nitrogen is not harmful, but due to instability some of the nitrate turns to nitrite, and it is only the latter form that is lethal. Is the nitrate in organically grown vegetables more stable? That is something which has not been proven.

There is a vast amount of research that proves unquestionably that too much nitrogen in a plant opens it up to a host of diseases and conditions. One writer refers to how plants may go on a "nitrogen jag." He describes an experiment with rabbits which were given an opportunity to eat grasses treated with varying amounts of nitrogen. They always avoided grass that was grown with too much nitrogen, leaving it to the very last and consuming it only to avoid starvation.

There is evidence that a large amount of nitrogen encourages the production of soft, succulent tissue which bruises more easily and is susceptible to the attack of disease—mildew, verticillium wilt, virus infections, et cetera. The evidence is too conclusive to be ignored.

In conclusion, on this point of too much compost, you might ask: "Are you attempting to break down the organic method?" I would reply, "No. I am attempting to strengthen it by maintaining an open mind." This is merely an exploratory bit of writing. I am not going to take too definite a stand on the subject. Let us check and observe and decide later. Why kill yourself by lugging too much organic matter for your compost heap? Bear in mind that as the store of humus in your soil rises there will be an increase of the earthworms and soil micro-organisms. They will do part of the job for you. Let us not overdo a good thing.

TWELVE

MULCHING

Mulching means the piling up of organic matter—such as grass clippings, weeds, leaves—around growing plants, usually done to a height of ten or twelve inches. In the case of potatoes, however, the mulch can be applied immediately upon planting, before anything has come out of the ground, since the young plant has no trouble working its way up through the green matter. We have found this an excellent method of growing this tuber, and for some strange reason we have noticed no infestation of potato bugs when we have mulched in this fashion. In other cases we would apply the mulch after the plant has grown somewhat.

The purpose of mulching, mainly, is to conserve the moisture in the topsoil. You will see this quite graphically when you mulch. Whereas open ground is dry and arid in hot weather, the soil under a covering of organic matter is dark and moist. At the end of the growing season you can dig the mulch into the soil, thus providing food and sustenance for next year's crop.

Many gardeners use this as their only method of applying fertilizer, making no compost. It is suggested, however, in such cases that some animal matter be mixed into the mulch material, such as dried blood, bone meal, tankage, or some manure. Thus you have a composting mixture as a mulch. If this is not practical, a separate dressing of manure can be dug in at the end of the growing season.

Mulching is a good way of making compost, for the material decays in a cold decomposition, not with the high heat of a compost heap which oxidizes out valuable nutrients, bacteria, enzymes, et cetera. Then when the material is dug in, there is that dynamic action which has been described in a previous chapter. There is a steady stream of nutrients going off when they are needed for the growth requirements of the next crop.

All mulch material should be thoroughly dug in at the end of the summer so as not to furnish a winter haven for certain undesirable insects who like to use such plant matter for that purpose. One layer of mulch which starts at about twelve inches and goes down to about two or three at the end of the season should not be an excessive amount of organic matter to give the soil each year.

Mulching and Potassium

There is extensive literature to indicate that there is production of potassium under a mulch. In one test a type of mulch which was low in potassium was used on a soil in which the potassium tested low. After the elapse of a period of time, the soil tested much higher in potash, much more than would be warranted by the amount of potash in the plant material of the mulch. Evidently the leaching down into the soils of liquids obtained from the mulch furnished something that worked on the insoluble potash in the soil and made some of it available.

Carbon dioxide given off in plant matter decay may have been a factor. When compost is made, large amounts of carbon dioxide are given off and lost into the atmosphere. This shows the advantage of making "compost" directly on the soil which is the scene of the planting activities. It does many things of value to the soil.

Difficulties in Mulching

Mulching may sometimes prove dangerous in the early season when there is risk of freezing. At such a time the mulch increases the warmth under it, and if the weather turns too cold, the upper part of the plant may freeze. This has happened often in England, where they try for a long growing season. Where there is such a question, and if there is a mulch on the ground, rake it aside into piles, but be sure to keep these piles on unplanted portions of the patch so that liquid leachings from them will be preserved in soil where planting is done. Where new mulch material is accumulated, make piles of it, if possible, right in the vegetable garden, for the same reason. If it is a dry year or a dry region, water should be applied to the mulch.

Difficulties in mulching peas and lettuce have been reported. In extremely wet weather the mulch must be pulled away so that it does not touch the stems of the plants. Hay from winter rye should not be used as a mulch on strawberry plants, reports the Connecticut Agricultural Experiment Station.

Varied Experiences

One of our readers in North Carolina had an interesting experience in pre-mulching tomatoes. First he plowed and harrowed, then he mulched the ground with about six to eight inches of wheat straw. Then, using Rutgers plants, he set his tomato plants through the mulch at a distance of four feet apart each way. To set the plants he pulled the mulch apart and set the roots in the prepared ground, then pushed the mulch back together around the stems. This was the end of his work. He did nothing else the entire season but pick tomatoes. Dark green vines soon completely covered and obliterated the mulch. No weeds grew. There was an immense set of fine tomatoes which remained large, with hardly any culls, throughout the growing season, and the vines were still full of tomatoes at frost. Because of the fact that the fruit rested on the straw mulch, there was scarcely any rotting at any time during the season.

Another reader writes: "I am accomplishing wonders with my roses through the use of finely ground peanut hulls mixed with old compost. I use a small concrete mixer—fill it with the ground peanut hulls, add the compost, then enough water to thoroughly dampen it—then mulch the beds and keep them mulched. The high alkalinity is steadily going down. I have quit composting entirely."

The *Annapolis Valley Post Road,* a magazine published in Nova Scotia, dated May 15, 1950, said:

"Herbert and Edward Fairn, members of the Round Hill Fruit Co., Ltd., are situated close to an abundant supply of rich organic fertilizer. Seaweed, valued for many years as a fertilizer in coastal regions of Europe, is available within easy carting distance of their orchard.

"Herbert Fairn stated recently that a heavy seaweed mulch has produced excellent results. Used experimentally in a block of Wagener trees, at the rate of six hundred pounds per tree, the seaweed was credited with decided improvement in the quality of the fruit. Mr. Fairn also declared that the mulch had resulted in improved keeping quality. The trees had made excellent growth. In fact, growth had been so rank in certain cases that he considered it inadvisable to bring in seaweed the following year."

One experiment showed that mulching apple trees tended to make them bear annually instead of every other year.

The following excerpt from the Journal of the Soil Association of England, *Mother Earth*, Winter 1947–48, shows that mulching reduced insect infestation:

"A fruit-grower friend of mine never cultivates now between his soft fruit, but just slashes down the grass and leaves it to rot *in situ*, without ever letting it get tall enough to choke the bushes. This summer he has had no attacks from greenfly, etc., and, incidentally, no big bud on his black currants. No spraying was done."

Caution: Many people have a passion for keeping the beds under shrubbery immaculately clean. They will clean out pine needles, for example, in order to compost them. This is a great mistake and sometimes leads to disease in the trees. Nature allows the pine needles to accumulate under her trees and make a nice bed of mulch, furnishing a continuous supply of humus and protecting the surface of the soil from baking.

Here is a little note that appeared in a magazine called *Fruit Notes:*

"During a ten-year study of a Michigan pear orchard of the Bartlett variety, more fire blight was observed in a clean culture-cover crop than in a sod-mulch plot. Blight infections were also more frequently fatal to trees during their vigorously growing, non-bearing years than similar infections during later years. As the trees came into bearing and growth became less vigorous and succulent, they became more resistant to the invasion and rapid movement of the blight organism. The decrease in growth and succulence of twigs was hastened by the competition of the sod cover for moisture and mineral nutrients in the sod-mulch plot, thereby encouraging a type of growth resistant to blight infection."

Buckwheat hulls make an excellent mulch for flowers and give the beds a neat appearance. Mulched roses are freer of disease than unmulched, says one authority. There is much to be learned yet about mulching. The gardener must be on the alert and be ready to make adjustment when he sees a need for it.

THIRTEEN

SOIL CONDITIONERS

A new product has recently come upon the agricultural scene which has the horticultural world exclaiming and is making agricultural writers crow in happy excitement about it. One writer heads his description, *The Desert Shall Blossom*. Another says, *Magic Soil Chemical Does Everything but Can Fruit*. There are titles like, *Science Harnesses Atom for Humanity, Synthetic Restores Soil Productivity in Hours, Wonder Drug Restores Sick Soil*, and dozens of other loud and joyous hosannas about this and that soil conditioner which is supposed to spell the doom of organic matter as a soil supplement.

These conditioners are supposed to take the most refractory of hard, clay-packed soils and restore their open structure, giving them good tilth, making them soft, friable, and well-granulated, enabling them to absorb adequate rainfall, aerating the roots of plants and giving them power to better penetrate the soil. They are supposed to make cultivation easier, to stimulate

the activity of soil organisms, permitting the soil to breathe better. This, it is claimed, means that plants will grow better and
thus there will be higher yields. And all in twenty-four hours!
That's the twentieth century for you—no waiting, no delays, no
backbreaking digging for the gardener.

I like the way *Business Week* magazine describes what one
of these soil conditioners will do. It says, "Essentially, Agrilon
takes over the job that worms would have done if they hadn't
been killed by chemical fertilizers." This appeared in their May
4, 1952, issue, page 60. So they admit that the use of chemical
fertilizers kills the earthworms! When did this change-over in
belief occur? Personally, I'll take the earthworm when I see that
it adds at least five tons of castings per acre per year on my
farm without my stirring a finger or spending a penny in labor
for it.

The rush by companies to get into this bonanza is taking on
all the appearances of the old gold-rush days. There is Krilium,
Loamium, Fluffium, Agrigair, Terrakem, Crosoil, Aerisoil, CMC,
Aerotil, Soilife, Soiloam, Merloam, Poly-ack, Ackril, Agrilon,
and Soil Conditioner W. By tomorrow there will be a hundred
more. Fluffium expected to do seven million dollars' worth of
business in its first year. Whether or not it did so, I will never
know.

As I stand off and look at the scurrying merchant chemists,
it reminds me of a farmer who had a broken-down barn, all
the timbers of which were in an advanced state of rotting. A
salesman talked him into sheathing the whole outside of it with
nice white asbestos shingles, and he did so. The place took on
a most attractive appearance, but a few years later the whole
thing collapsed, because no attention was paid to the basic functional aspects of certain parts of the structure. I wonder if that
is going to be the story of these conditioners.

High Cost of Conditioners

As it stands now, the cost of the material is so high that the manufacturers recommend it only for gardeners. A farmer would have to pay as high as three thousand dollars an acre to apply the stuff, and the average farm land costs only a small fraction of that. But the gardener is much better off to forget all this nonsense and spend the same money for peat or humus. Then he really has something. He does not have to lie awake at night wondering what is going to happen in his plot of soil fifteen years later.

There are many limitations to these soil conditioners. They work only in clay soils. But do you think that sandy soils do not have similar problems, that sandy soils do not develop hard-pans? Neither do these conditioners improve loam or muck soils.

The average conditioner is called an organic chemical, but don't let that lull you. It is organic in the sense that aspirin, which is made from coal tar, is organic. The conditioner is a resin made from natural gas and ammonia. If it is composed of substances powerful enough to change the structure of matter so quickly, I believe it is a dangerous thing to play with.

In advertising literature companies claim that these conditioners are non-toxic at the rates of application advised. But suppose a fellow grows carrots and by mistake uses too much of the soil conditioners? I have also heard the word *non-toxic* misused a great deal. A company, in its sales literature, says that a certain chemical is harmless to human beings. But my file of medical information sometimes indicates otherwise. The company is after dividends. The stockholder is a hard task-master.

In dentistry a resin in the same family as the new soil conditioners is being used as a filling for cavities—it is a methyl methacrylate, called an acrylic resin. I have before me an article from the March 1952 issue of the *Journal of the American Dental Association* which says, "The expansion and contraction of the direct filling resins during changes in mouth temperature cause the ingress and egress of liquids along the filling margin —a weakness that may predispose to recurrent caries." You see, in dentistry, also, a thing looks like magic and it is rushed into use before there is sufficient time to discover its shortcomings. In the same article it stated that some of the new plastics used for tooth fillings caused harmful reactions in the tooth pulp.

Admitted Negative Aspects

We are beginning to hear a few negative things "in the trade" about these soil conditioners. The Ohio State Flower Growers' Association reported as follows at their recent annual short course as quoted from *Grower Talks:*

"Krilium was the next subject—this is the soil aggregator which makes small soil particles cling together into larger groups. This gets back to the very important and fundamental problem of handling greenhouse soils in such a way that they will remain porous, well drained, and well aerated. Any grower knows how vitally important this is to good production. The big disappointment here was that, while scientific measurements proved that Krilium did force the small soil particles to get together, yet in terms of roses produced, the Krilium did no good whatever. Actually, manure was more effective."

At the Connecticut Agricultural Experiment Station, in experiments with Krilium, harmful effects were shown in growing geraniums. This was written up by Dr. C. L. Swanson, the chief soil scientist of that station, in the *Journal of Soil and Water Conservation* for April 1952:

"Mysteriously, in the Connecticut experiments the geraniums potted in soil treated with Krilium developed root rot. Roots of those plants, in fact, were almost non-existent and the plants themselves looked quite sick. Geranium cuttings planted in plain soil grew vigorously and with fine roots."

Of the plants in the Krilium-treated soil, 18 per cent died and half had no roots showing. None showed normal development. Dr. Swanson did not know exactly why Krilium caused such harm to geraniums, but he hazards the guess that Krilium caused the soil to become too well aerated, producing an increase in nitrogen uptake which possibly smothered the plants' ability to take up potassium.

Dr. Swanson uncovered another even more fantastic result of the use of Krilium. He found that when a soil that is treated with Krilium is allowed to dry out completely, water is unable to penetrate. Rain runs off as though the soil were concrete. Although soil out in the open seldom dries out completely, that condition is met with in greenhouses, says Dr. Swanson.

Soil Conditioners and Soil Erosion

Regarding the prevention of soil erosion by Krilium, Dr. William Chepil, Kansas State College agronomy professor who has just finished a year's research on it, has found, according to the May 18, 1952, issue of the Topeka *Daily Capitol,* that:

"In small amounts, the new compound has not reduced soil erosion by wind. It tends to aggregate finer silts and clay particles and creates a porous structure in the soil with no surface crusting. This helps prevent soil erosion from water, but the untreated soils form a surface crust that aids in preventing soil blowing more than the treated soils."

Dr. William Albrecht of the University of Missouri, in a letter to us regarding Krilium, said:

"Krilium might be effective in helping the plant obtain more fertility out of the soil. It is a tool for additional soil extraction or exploitation and not necessarily a tool from the common viewpoint of rebuilding the soil. Now it might make the application of our soil treatments more effective, if we applied those. But of itself it does not add fertility essentials to the soil. It is a fine tool to help us do some research in the changes in the structure of the soil and just exactly what they mean.

"I fear, however, that in the final analysis the use of this material will merely tell us that we are removing the exchangeable materials from the clay of the soil that much faster because of this extra aeration and the better granulation."

A special writer in the June 22, 1952, issue of the *Milwaukee Journal,* in a feature article entitled "Companies Fight It Out Over Soil Conditioners," talks about a "flurry of rather extravagant claims" for these synthetics. "The merit of soil conditioners has flared into a war of words, claims, pictures, and demonstrations involving multimillion-dollar corporations, small chemical companies, mail-order houses, wholesalers, and retailers. All are eager to capture the home garden market and attract the dollars of farmers. The feud is but a phase of a mighty word controversy that has been raging in agriculture for some time—organic farming versus commercial fertilizers."

Conditioners Cause Soil Destruction

In our opinion the basic drawback of the use of these soil conditioners is that it would educate the farmer and gardener to ignore completely the value of organic matter to the well-being of the soil. It sets up a condition where the small store of soil humus is used up more quickly. Where it is used on a soil that is infertile to begin with, it will create sterile conditions which will require increasing amounts of chemical fertilizer. It makes the artificial system of farming and gardening more artificial.

The use of these soil conditioners completely overlooks the nutritional needs of food crops and the fact that the public is entitled to as much vitamin content in their produce as it is possible to grow into it. Soil conditioners are crutches that are being added to the other crutches of our dubious artificial agricultural systems.

Soil conditioners are a part of the march of artificial practices which are becoming more artificial each year. They could not have come into existence without having been preceded, step by step and technique by technique, with untested theories and methods which have become more standard and acceptable with mere passage of time, but whose real value is absolutely questionable.

First there were artificial fertilizers. Then came pesticides and weedicides. There are systemic poison sprays that saturate every cell of a plant. We hear of stilbestrol, which sterilized minks, being used for fattening capons, and penicillin being used to add dubious weight on sheep. There is artificial insemination of cattle, and artificial pollination of fruit blossoms because the bees are being killed off by the spray poisons. There are chemicals used to make fruit hang on the branch for dear life and other chemicals to make them drop off. There are chemicals to force sheep to have twins whether their bodies are adjusted to it or not. Everything is artificial or chemically induced. The soil conditioners, therefore, had to come. It is part of the NPK mentality (nitrogen-phosphorus-potash).

CHEMICAL FERTILIZERS

There is a vehement controversy raging in regard to the question, *Shall chemical fertilizers be used?* This, however, should be broken down into two parts—as it affects the farmer and as it affects the gardener—for in regard to the latter no one who will take four or five weeks to grow a few flowers or vegetables can fail to discover that there is only one way to garden, and that is not with commercial fertilizers. Applying the method in farming, of course, takes a bit of doing. To gain adherents in that division of horticulture, one must discuss, argue, bring proof of higher yields, less disease, et cetera. But in gardening? It is like swimming with the tide. Any gardening writer who holds a brief for the use of chemical fertilizers either has not tried the organic method or is not writing in good faith.

If you will go back to Chapter Two, "The Soil," you will note that the soil is made up of organic matter, minerals, water, and air, and it is only common sense not to intrude any other elements. If you have ever had the pleasure of growing anything organically or visited an organic garden, your eyes will tell you that these four things can do the job beautifully as far as yield is concerned. Such tremendous cabbages! Such lettuces! In fact, any vegetables grow in such abundant lushness that the neighbors think magic is being practiced.

Solubility of Chemical Fertilizers

The trouble with most chemical fertilizers is that they are manufactured products in which usually some chemical has been added for the sole purpose of making the nutrients in the fertilizer more soluble. Solubility is the opposite of inertness. Chemically speaking, it means that the substance is in solution, that it can be taken up easily, that it is available to the plant. You can almost compare it to inert iron which, when it is heated above its melting point, begins to flow. Chemical fertilizers are too much "on the flow." They are "flowing" all the time, and the plant has to take it whether it wants to or not. This is especially true when it comes to potassium. Some plants are drunkards when it comes to that element, and if any soluble potassium is around they will drink it up. But too much potassium may be actually dangerous for some plants—from one point of view especially, potassium is a factor in creating carbohydrates. Thus imbalances come about. In my garden I want Nature to be the chef, to mix the ingredients, to determine the correct proportions of carbohydrates, proteins, minerals, and vitamins. I use organic matter and rock powders which "flow" at a slower rate, but yet in sufficient quantity to give me asparagus, Brussels sprouts, et cetera. My plants don't want to start growing with too much of a rush and then slow down. In our method it is the story of the hare and the tortoise. The plants go at an even pace, but when all is said and done you have more, both in volume and in quality, than the chemically run plants.

Now, in order to get this fast flow, strange elements are added to the chemical fertilizer compounds—sulphates, sodas, and chlorides. The plants do not need much of them. These items are used merely to make the other parts of the fertilizer "flow" or be soluble. Therefore each year they keep piling up in the soil. After seven or eight years of using chemical fertilizers, you wake up one fine morning, or one growing season, and suddenly discover that things "ain't what they used to be," no matter how much you spray. You still have Mexican bean beetle. Your tomatoes get fungus, crack easily, and just don't taste good any more. This is not propaganda. It is fact, and you can easily prove it for yourself.

One of the greatest advantages of the organic method is that each year you are adding something to your soil that gives it a spongelike quality, that makes it sop up the rain water, that gives it a good structure or tilth. It gives you the supremest pleasure to regard the wonderful darkness of your soil, to run your hand through its softness. Because of this, in a year of drought the contrast between an organic garden and the neighbor's chemical one becomes so startlingly noticeable that if they don't take the hint there is something wrong somewhere.

Disadvantages of Chemical Fertilizers

There are many other disadvantages in using chemical fertilizers. For one thing, they kill earthworms, and every earthworm in the soil is worth its weight many times over. Chemicals tend to burn out the needed humus of the soil. They inactivate the protective antibiotic organisms and beneficial bacteria. They harden the soil and make it difficult to pull out weeds. There is much better aeration under the organic method. There is less disease and not so many insects. No poison sprays need be used. The crop tastes better and makes people who eat it healthier.

A very decided disadvantage of using chemicals is the confusion regarding their usage. For instance, one authority says that the fertilizer should not be applied too heavily in a dry year. How is one to know it is going to be a dry year?

A reader asks his gardening magazine for advice. His tomato plants grow tall without ripening fruit. He is told that his soil contains too much nitrogen and not enough phosphorus. So he will go hard on the phosphorus. Next year his plants will suffer from symptoms of an oversupply of phosphorus. The fact is that there is no one formula for tomatoes. The April 1944 issue of *Farm Research,* a Cornell University publication, states, "In fertilizer experiments with cannery tomatoes it has been demonstrated that no one formula can be recommended for all soils. The highest yields were obtained from the highest nitrogen ratio on Ontario loam at Geneva, from the highest amount of phosphorus on Fulton silty clay at Fredonia, and from the heaviest potash application on Palmyra gravelly loam at Marion." In the organic method you are not fettered by formulas. A certain amount of organic matter, a reasonable amount of rock powders, and the soil will answer back with more than you reckon.

Here is a statement from a publication issued by the N. Y. State Agricultural Experiment Station at Geneva, N.Y. "Some fertilizers are very toxic and inhibit root growth, while others stimulate root development. Some fertilizers are quite inert, some are slow-acting, and others dissolve quickly and give immediate growth response." You do not know how they will affect your particular requirements.

Overuse of Chemicals

Many gardeners use too much chemical fertilizer because of a lack of knowledge of the make-up of these strong chemicals. In *North-West Gardens* (June 1944 issue) there is a warning which is given herewith: "Because commercial fertilizers are so highly concentrated, they must not be allowed to come in contact with the plant, so a trench is dug from two to four inches away from the stems. Also, care must be taken to remove immediately any that may be spilled on the leaves, for if allowed to remain, burning may result. Many gardeners do not realize the potency of commercial fertilizers and use far too much. This is both dangerous and wasteful; dangerous because roots can be burned by large amounts not properly blended with the soil, and wasteful because plants can only take up so much food at a time, and when too heavy an application of fertilizer is made, a large portion leaches away before the plants can use it. It is far better to apply small amounts more often."

This reminds me of the experience of my wonderful brother Joe. When he first began to garden he bought a bag of a popular brand of commercial fertilizer and applied it evenly over his whole garden according to instructions. However, he found himself with half a bag left over and, figuring that it might spoil over the winter, gave his garden a double dose. Result? A terrible garden that year.

It is much safer to use natural ingredients—the same things that Nature uses in her gardening. Nature is an experienced soil chemist. She works deftly and harmoniously. She mixes her brews with an experience stemming from a background of millions of years. Say what you will, man rarely figures out his discoveries from a preconceived theoretical plan. They result either by accident or by trial and error. Nature went through the trial-and-error stage millions of years ago. Man is still in the swaddling clothes of this principle. His use of chemistry in farming is just one example of his method of applying his "science." He is floundering about in a sea of chemical uncertainty.

Man throws an excess of potassium in the soil and is not aware that this precipitates the soil magnesium. Magnesium is badly needed, lack of it causing diseases in rye and oats. In Alabama it was found that on certain clay soils the application of phosphates caused iron chlorosis. Man sprays the soil and unknowingly there accumulates in that soil, arsenic, copper, lead, and zinc, which after a while prevent even cover crops in orchards from growing. Trial and error, but mostly error.

Purchasable Organic Fertilizers

Chemical fertilizers are expensive. For the same amount of money you can buy enough compost to go six times as far. If you are not disposed to make compost, you can purchase it. In addition to compost there is already available on the market, at regular garden-supply stores, a variety of manufactured or mixed products that contain no concentrated, too soluble chemical ingredients. There is Soil-Til, Atlas fish fertilizer, dried seaweed, Espoma, greensand, Gro-mulch, Nu-Erth, Orgamin, worm castings, Driconure, guano, Green nitro, ground leaf mold, leather dust, and a host of others. And the list is growing fast. Even the big American Agricultural Chemical Company, the firm that makes chemical fertilizers, recently has placed an all-organic fertilizer on the market.

Letters from Readers

We receive hundreds of letters from readers of *Organic Gar-*

dening who in glowing superlatives, for which you cannot blame them, describe how much more they get in yield of vegetables from organic fertilizers than from the use of chemicals. There is so much evidence of this kind that there cannot be the slightest doubt on this point. Here are a few typical letters:

PAUL B. GOODIER
Carmichael, Calif., Aug. 1953

"Our Sweet Meat squash were something to behold. The seed catalog stated the size as from eight to ten pounds. Most all of ours weighed from thirty-five to forty-three pounds each, and one vine produced over three hundred forty pounds of sweet, high-quality, long-keeping squash. We may have fresh squash until the new summer crop.

"Our melons were the best we had ever eaten. One man, a visitor from Pittsburgh, Pa., after purchasing a couple of our Crenshaws, came back and begged us to let him have two more to take back home to Pittsburgh to his folks to show them his find and what real organic melons were like. He took them by plane and I hope they arrived safely. I asked him if they didn't grow good melons back there and he said, 'Well, I always thought we did, but I've never tasted anything like these before.'

"I could go on and on telling you of our experiences, such as our County Farm Advisor's reactions to our garden soybeans. When they were a little over half grown I pulled up one vine and took it to town to inquire of him what, if anything, might be wrong with the roots, which proved to be no more than a beginner's worries about nothing. But the point is, he first asked me what kind of plants they were and he just couldn't believe this specimen was a soybean. He said, 'Soybeans are not supposed to grow that large, and if anything is wrong with the roots, such a strong plant will overcome it anyway.' But he said,

'The important question is, will you get any beans from them? They seem too rank of growth to produce beans.' He added that commercial growers have not been able to produce worthwhile crops of soybeans in the Sacramento Valley for some reason, and for me not to be disappointed.

"When these soybeans were through growing they were over my head, topping six feet, and the crop seemed to be endless. We ate all we could fresh, canned enough for a couple of seasons, and then called in the neighbors to pick all they wanted, and still rototilled under probably a third of the crop. Three cheers for Organics!"

FLOYD WILBANKS
Logansport, Ind., Jan. 1953

"I have been growing berries the organic way for several years. When other growers of berries are drying up in July, mine are as fresh then as at the first of the season. During the winter I haul much of my material. Leaves from the city dump, manures from riding stables, chicken farms, sheep raisers, and grow cover crops. I gather these materials from September till June. Sometimes I drive fifteen miles, but I have proven it is worth it.

"I will raise as much on one of my acres as some will on three. I get eight thousand to ten thousand quarts to the acre and that ain't HAY."

MRS. LEE J. ANDERSON
Coachella, Calif., 1950

"We certainly had startling proof of the value of organiculture last fall. Dates require hot days and cool nights during September and October to mature naturally. An unusually hot spell through these two months caused the dates which had not been properly nurtured to dry up on the palm so that all required picking by mid-November. Our organically grown dates continued to mature normally and we were still picking dates as late as February.

"We wish you continued success in disseminating your valuable information."

FIFTEEN

THE FERTILIZERS THAT NATURE GIVES US

It has been shown in a previous chapter that it is not necessary to push the soil too much with regard to compost. An aspect of this subject which was not taken up there was the ability of the soil to fend for itself. The gardener, if he is to enjoy his hobby to the full, should be familiar with the whole cycle of knowledge in regard to what makes his plants grow. The ability of the soil to furnish him free fertilizer is one of the most interesting little cogs in that wheel. The gardener should be aware of the amazing fact that plants get only from 2 to 5 per cent of their nourishment from the soil. The remainder comes from the air. In other words, the soil is not a closed system that is self-contained; it is only a small part of a much bigger whole. A host of fertilizer material comes free of charge out of the rest of the whole, provided the soil is in the proper condition of receptivity. But if the soil has been soured up and hard-packed by the overuse of strong chemical fertilizers, then much of it will be lost.

Let us take the case of the bacteria themselves. In a very fertile soil their weight per acre may be as high as six hundred pounds. When they die, their decaying bodies immediately turn to rich humus. When you consider how fast they multiply and die, the annual contribution from this source must be no mean sum. But the richer the soil in organic matter, the greater is this total. When the fertilizer emphasis is mainly on chemicals much less help may be expected from this source.

Free Nitrogen

Most of us are aware that when we grow leguminous plants, such as peas or soybeans, there are organisms living in nodules in their roots that enrich the soil with nitrogen which they extract from the soil air. But most of us are not aware that there are other organisms—bacteria, algae, and possibly even fungi —that are free-acting: that is, not working in connection with the roots of any plants, but continually deriving nitrogen from the air. Lyon and Buckman, in their book, *Nature and Properties of Soils*, describe the actions and abilities of these microorganisms. According to the authors, these bacteria are dependent on the supply of organic matter for their energy. The nitrogen extracted from the air is incorporated into their bodies and given to the soil upon their death. The bacteria group that does this is the Azotobacter, and the process is called azofication.

In England an experiment covering a period of twenty years produced forty-four pounds of nitrogen per acre yearly, and the plants grown were non-legumes. At Cornell University, in an experiment where the plots were kept in continuous grass, the cuttings being plowed under as organic fertilizer, azofication yielded forty-two pounds per acre. But on plots where the grass cuttings were taken off, only between fifteen and twenty pounds of nitrogen was obtained from the air by soil micro-organisms. It can be seen, therefore, that where a soil becomes extremely rich in humus, the azotobacter and other free-acting, nitrogen-gathering micro-organisms multiply, and thus much more than forty-two pounds of nitrogen should be obtainable from this source per acre every year. Organic matter is the ideal medium to make bacteria thrive and multiply. It is their food and gives them the energy to work. It has been found by experiment also that where there is a sufficient supply of chemical fertilizer nitrogen, these bacteria turn their attention to it and use it as the source of nitrogen, neglecting the supply contained in the air.

The legume plants—beans, peas, alfalfa, soybeans, clover, et cetera—have the ability to take nitrogen from the air in large amounts, storing it in the soil about their roots for future use. Scientists have found that a good stand of legumes will bring from the air about fifty pounds of nitrogen per acre per year, although there have been cases of two hundred pounds per acre being obtained.

Fifty pounds of nitrogen per acre is the equivalent of two hundred pounds of nitrate of soda, so you can see how much better it is to depend on the natural methods of securing free fertilizing materials. Besides, when nitrate of soda is used, much of the soda keeps on piling up in the soil and causes it to harden and lose its structure. One investigator found that legume plants obtained two thirds of their total nitrogen requirements from the air. It is a known fact, however, that when Cyanamid, a chemical fertilizer, is used it inactivates the nitrogen-fixing bacteria in the soil.

The Earthworm Provides Fertilizer

Let us take the earthworm as another example of free fertilizer. By actual count it has been discovered that where synthetic fertilizers are used the angleworm population declines, sometimes almost to the vanishing point. Now this beneficent earth worker has a very short life span, probably not more than a year or two, so that in a fertile soil hundreds of thousands of them are dying per acre each year. Can you conceive of a more valuable fertilizer material than the dead bodies of these creatures? It has been stated that such dead bodies may amount to tons per acre per year, and this consists of the most wonderful protein, as well as valuable mineral matter of the highest quality for plant nutrition. In such a fertile soil the microbes will break such bodies down and make the matter almost instantly available for the feeding of plant roots. A few hundred pounds of dead bacteria per acre added to the weight of dead earthworms should be a wonderful source of live fertilizer material.

The earth is teeming with other life—spiders, beetles, ants, moles, and so forth. Their excreta and their dead bodies must enrich the soil to a considerable degree. But surely chemical fertilizers and poison sprays must kill off some of them. In England comparative experiments showed that soils where chemical fertilizers were used contained much less insect life than where the organic method was practiced. We will show in a later chapter that by the organic method disease organisms and destructive insects are kept in safe, biologic adjustment and control.

Then there is the excremental matter voided by these insects and earthworms. In the case of the latter, Darwin has estimated that it amounts to ten tons an acre. Others have given figures as high as twenty-five tons. I believe these estimates to be too high, but surely it must amount to a considerable sum. The Connecticut Experimental Station found that these earthworm castings contained five times as much nitrogen as that contained in the topsoil, seven times as much magnesium. The picture is building up rather nicely, don't you think? But this isn't the half of it. Nature still has more tricks up her sleeve.

Roots of Plants as Fertilizer

One of the most valuable sources of organic matter in the soil is the dead roots of old plants. In the case of a two-year-old crop of red clover these roots amounted to over three tons per acre and were found to contain one hundred eighty pounds of nitrogen, seventy-one pounds of phosphorus, and seventy-seven pounds of potash. Roots, not being too bulky, decay readily, and the places they occupied remain as channels to aerate the subsoil. On the average, the roots amount to about half the weight of the entire crop. It has been shown that the roots of organically grown plants are much heavier than those grown with chemical fertilizers, one reason being that the soil is aerated much better. Oxygen is extremely important to root activity. The consideration of root residues does not take into consideration the above-ground residues of crops, which in some cases would amount to two or three tons per acre of the finest fertilizer material. This green matter contains everything needed in the plant's nutrition.

Also we should not overlook the mycorrhiza fungus in the treatment of this subject. This is an organism that attaches itself to the roots of plants and finds food in the soil which it gives up to the plant. This is known as a symbiotic relationship between the mycorrhiza and the root—that is, each helps the other. But in the final stages of plant growth the roots consume the fungus. This is a very valuable plant-feeding mechanism, but it has been found that where chemical fertilizers are used either the mycorrhiza is absent or much reduced in amount. Evidently this fungus works on inert minerals in the soil and makes them "available" to the plant. Thus, by merely having sufficient organic matter in his soil, the organic gardener gains the aid of a valuable ally that creates something out of nothing, because the inert mineral is absolutely valueless unless it is transformed into a usable condition.

Lightning and Rain as Fertilizing Agents

Another free form of fertilizer is lightning. Every time lightning strikes the earth large amounts of nitrogen are charged into the ground. Engineers of the Westinghouse Electric Corporation have shown that in a single year more nitrogen is given to the ground through lightning than is manufactured commercially in the entire world in that period. The lightning discharge seems to decompose the water vapor in the air and, in so doing, makes new combinations of oxygen and nitrogen. One authority states that two hundred fifty thousand tons of natural nitrogen are produced every day of the year in the eighteen hundred thunderstorms that are always taking place somewhere or other on this earth. One agricultural authority says that nitrogen from this source may amount in some places to more than ten pounds per acre per year.

The rain brings with it much in the way of free fertilizer. Nitrogen is washed down to the extent of about five to six pounds per acre yearly, and even falls on the soil on dry days, but to a much lesser extent. In some places it was found that rain brought down as high as twenty pounds per acre annually. This nitrogen is in a form that is readily available to plants. Snow furnishes not only nitrogen but also phosphorus and other minerals. That is why it has been referred to as the poor man's manure. I recall reading somewhere that in the late spring the grass was much greener where snowdrifts had been in mounds.

At other parts of the field the June grass was sparse and brown. If you have the time, it is not a bad idea to shovel snow onto your compost heaps.

Sulphur is another valuable element that comes down with the rain. Studies have been made which show that at least forty pounds of sulphur are washed into the soil per acre per year. This quantity must be greater on farms which are located near industrial cities where the smoke contains much sulphur. It has recently been shown by experiments in Florida in a government experimental station that sulphur is absolutely necessary in connection with the growing of oranges. But at the very end of a long pamphlet in which the entire details of this experiment were demonstrated, and the disastrous consequences of a lack of this element shown, it was mentioned casually that the orange grower need not worry about the lack of sulphur because "there is a sufficient quantity of it in the air which is washed into the earth every time it rains. This takes care of the earth's normal sulphur requirements."

Rain water also contains carbonic acid, which forms into carbon dioxide in the soil and which is needed in the soil and plant feeding relationship. Millions of tons of carbonic acid fall yearly on the soil. Nearly half the make-up of a plant is carbon. There seems to be evidence that many rare minerals, such as selenium and molybdenum, are washed down in the rain.

Dust

Dust coming down upon the soil is an item not to be disregarded, since it contains minerals, organic matter, and beneficial micro-organisms. In the fine dust thrown off by volcanic eruptions there are large amounts of organic matter, sometimes running as high as from 25 to 34 per cent. Ordinary dust also contains substantial quantities of minerals essential to plant growth. It is said that much of the richness of the land in Central American and East Indian countries is directly attributable to this distribution of dust. The dust, floating thousands upon thousands of miles—often held suspended for years in the upper atmosphere—is finally brought to earth by moisture-filled air or by rain itself. The fogs, also, contribute to the soil's fertility. Along the seacoast these fogs bring in large quantities of iodine, nitrogen, and chlorine.

Investigators showed that the soil of Swiss Alpine meadows was actually formed by dust from nearby mountains. They measured amounts of two to almost four pounds per square yard of dust that fell on an average each year. It is believed that dust is a most significant factor in restoring exhausted minerals to the soil and also contains much-needed bacteria that are so important for healthy soil life and continue to inoculate it from this source.

Rocks

In the consideration of the wealth of free fertilizer materials, we must not overlook the rocks which underlie the soil's substrata and which are continually weathering to form new soil. But this merely offsets surface soil erosion. It is the loose rock near the surface that may be more valuable than is generally thought. It not only gently disintegrates to form fertilizer, but serves other valuable purposes, such as to provide warmth and aeration. You may be surprised to see marvelous crops of corn growing in fields strewn over with stones in great profusion. Many old books on agriculture caution gardeners against making a too clean seedbed by removing all small rocks.

Thus you see what is being done for your garden every day

through outside sources, and by this time you must be convinced that by running it on the organic basis you can be a factor in getting more from the outside than you otherwise would.

SIXTEEN

ROCK POWDERS

As we have seen, in the organic method of gardening we attempt to feed the soil with the same ingredients as those of which it is composed. Since the soil is made up of four things—organic matter, water, air, and inorganic minerals formed from rock fragments—we would stay on the safe side by seeing that it gets only these four things. This chapter will deal with the use of mineral rock powders as a safe fertilizer.

First of all, let us understand that one of the most popular chemical fertilizers is superphosphate, the basis of which is a rock powder—phosphate rock. In order to change its chemical nature so as to make it more soluble—that is, more "on the flow," so to speak—the ground rock is treated with sulphuric acid. As I understand it, the process consists of 50 per cent rock powder and 50 per cent sulphuric acid. Thus the rock is transformed into a chemical fertilizer. But why do this? The agronomists claim that the rock by itself is too slow-acting. However, experience shows otherwise. In the state of Illinois the rock has been used by farmers since 1900. In that state over 90 per cent of the phosphate used is in the form of phosphate rock. At the Connecticut Agricultural Experiment Station a granite rock dust was recently used for its potash in growing tobacco, compared with the chemical fertilizer form of potash, and the rock was demonstrated to be superior. At the U. S. Government Agricultural Experiment Center at Beltsville, Maryland, the phosphate rock powder gave excellent results which were summarized as follows: "Another money-saving discovery is the use of ground-up crude phosphate rock. . . . The plants get as much phosphorus as they need without the necessity of adding costly phosphates to the nutrient solution." This statement was quoted in the November 30, 1946, issue of the *Science News Letter*. On thousands of organic farms and gardens phosphate rock has been used for many years with similar results.

There is one potent reason why the chemical fertilizer superphosphate should not be used. The plant has a great need for phosphate but not much for the sulphur contained in the sulphuric acid. The result is that the sulphur keeps on piling up in the soil from year to year to the latter's detriment. When the gardener purchases an all-purpose commercial fertilizer with a brand name, or one with a number, such as 4-8-4, the middle number is the phosphate portion and usually consists of superphosphate, with its sulphur complement. Sulphur in more than its ordinary requirement has a deleterious effect on certain soil organisms which are needed to break down organic matter.

The Relation of Rock Powders and Organic Matter

Here is another important fact which is often overlooked: the more organic matter there is in a soil, the more readily will the rock powder particles be acted upon, to dissolve and go into solution—that is, to become available to plants. This is because in the decay of organic matter mild acids are produced, including carbonic acid, which aid in the dissolution of the rock particles. Naturally, in agricultural experiments where organic matter was not used in conjunction with the rock powder, under certain conditions, the results have not favored the latter. This is especially true where the soil is too alkaline. In such situations, by not using lime and by digging in adequate amounts of organic matter, the soil soon reverts to a form in which the rock powders can be made soluble in sufficient quantities for the needs of plants.

One of the reasons, probably, why the fallacy still persists that phosphate rock is not soluble is the fact that in the old days, when machinery was crude, the rock was not ground as fine as it is today. Nowadays it comes even finer than talcum powder. The smaller the particle, the easier its dissolution, naturally. But this rule does not hold true for all types of material. For example, in the case of wood, if it is in the form of ordinary sawdust, it will decay readily, but when it is in the form of woodflour, it is so fine that it tends to cake. Then decay is impeded. But rock is hard, and no matter how small the particle, it will not attach itself to another—it will not cake.

The Relation of Disease and Rock Underlayers

It has been discovered that the well-being of cattle and human beings is closely related to the kind of soil which grows their food, and this, in turn, is influenced by the kind of rock from which the soil is formed. Miscellaneous Publication No. 369 of the U. S. Department of Agriculture, entitled *The Mineral Composition of Crops* (out of print), represents a study and correlation of cases that point to the critical need for further investigation in this field.

According to Publication No. 369, the following rock formations are apt to weather into inferior soils:

Sandstones	Cretaceous rocks
Aplites	Air-borne pumice (an acid lava)
Granites	Volcanic
Pierre shales	

The better soils are on limestone, basalt, dolerite, diorite, and gabbro formations. With regard to gneiss soils, the results are sometimes good and at other times unfavorable. There are so many cases given that it is difficult to know where to begin to summarize. In Florida in 1931 a "salt sick" disease, an anemic condition of cattle, was found to occur in practically all parts of that state, but only on light, sandy soils. No such sickness occurred on clay soils. In New Zealand in 1932 it was found that bush sickness was found mostly over granite formations. A bone disease of livestock was discovered in Australia in 1895 in cattle fed largely from granite soils, where there was a deficiency of lime.

In 1920 there was a deficiency disease called "creeping sickness" in southern Alabama along the coastal plains; it was found only among people who lived on sandy soils low in lime content. In South Texas in 1924 there was a fatal disease in cattle called "loin disease" or "down-in-the-back," in a section where the soil was notably lime-deficient. A nutritional anemia in Florida was discovered in 1934 in the flatwoods country, affecting 96 per cent of the children in that section. The soil is known as Leon, and it is thin, sandy, and low in lime content. Six miles away, where the soil overlays hard rock phosphate, only 3 per cent of the children have this anemic condition. These are only a meager few of the cases mentioned in Publication No. 369, but they indicate a pressing need for a national survey of soil origins in connection with the incidence of human disease in each geologic formation.

Deaf Smith County, Texas, figured in the newspapers a few years ago when it became known as "the county without a toothache." The soil in Deaf Smith derives from rocks that are rich in lime and phosphorus and contain some fluorine, which is important in the making of bone and teeth. Even when strangers come to Deaf Smith County the cavities in their teeth glaze over and progress no further. The farmers bring in spindly cattle from Mexico and in a short time make fine, big-boned animals out of them. It is therefore important what kind of rock structure you have under your soil. It is a large factor in determining the nature of good soil.

It is advisable for a prospective purchaser of a farm to find out the rock percentage of its soil. This is seldom easy to determine categorically, as glacial limestone deposits are sometimes found or granite structures and other complex conditions may be detected. The purchaser can usually get good local advice from the county agricultural agent. The question may well be asked, "What shall I do if my farm happens to be located on one of the unfavorable soil formations?" Use liberal amounts of organic matter, lime, phosphate rock, dolomite, other rock powders, but none of the strong chemical fertilizers.

If you are really interested in knowing the full meaning of the place of rock powders in soil fertility, you can get more information from a book on elementary geology. Your library no doubt has many works on this subject, and there are a few books that deal specifically with the geology of agriculture. To really understand soil fertility you must be somewhat of a geologist.

The "Clean Culturists"

Many people believe that farming can be carried on without the use of animal manures. They call themselves *clean culturists* and their system is known as *clean culture*. This theory was first offered by Julius Hensel at Christiania, Norway, in 1885. He was against the use of manure and commercial fertilizers, advocating only finely ground-up rocks which he called *stone meal*. Some of the scientific professors sided with Hensel, others sneered, and a heated controversy flared up in the press. A few factories were erected to manufacture this stone meal, and in 1892 an exhibition was held in Leipzig, Germany, at which crops grown with this dust were shown. We would not advise any gardener to give up the use of manure. Over a long period, let us say ten to fifteen years, the soil would suffer from lack of it.

In 1924 Jack Gaerity, an American farmer, resurrected the work of Hensel and wrote a booklet based on it called *Bread and Roses from Stones*. In it he says, "Stone dust has been successfully used in England, but it faces the concrete wall of academic opposition there too. For several years, I am informed, a stone dust fertilizer has been on sale, under the trade name of 'Fluora.' The British Board of Agriculture, dominated by academic scientists, will not permit it to be sold as a fertilizer. It is distributed as a 'soil dressing.'" He states further, "J. A. Minchin, Esq., of Henfield, Sussex, states: 'I have, even this dry Summer (1919), grown most splendid salads with the aid of *Fluora*. My winter green stuff, Brussels sprouts, etc., are also looking remarkably well and strong.'"

Again he says, "B. Wettengel, a German farmer, writing in the *Wiesbadener General Anzeiger* of July 1, 1893, says, 'I have been using stone dust fertilizer in my garden and fields for five years. The results have always been satisfactory in every respect, for the soil becomes better every year by using this fertilizer. Especially this year, during the extraordinary drought, the excellent effects of stone dust fully manifested themselves. The flowers as well as the different vegetables developed so magnificently that every person who passed my garden stopped and admired the great growth, especially of the Kohlrabi.'" Gaerity says further, "Hundreds of British and German users might be quoted in praise of it. One quotation from each source, however, must suffice."

Our Rock Wealth

In the United States there is an enormous amount of rock. A survey might be made to ascertain special qualities in it, and tests made of the effect on the land. Some stone may have caustic properties and would have to be eliminated. Only those that are mild in action and that would not kill earthworms should be used. Charles Darwin, in his famous book on the earthworm, described how the worms swallow tiny rock particles which they grind up in their gizzards. With the use of powerful digestive juices they disintegrate tiny bits of rocks. They sift the finer from the coarser particles, and their castings make soil fit for the finest gardening. The earthworm, therefore, would be an invaluable ally where much pulverized rock would be applied to the soil. However, they could not live exclusively on it and would have to get organic material too.

In time to come more attention will be paid to the study of rocks and their possible use in agriculture. Rocks come in almost every color of the rainbow, and the colors are important clues to their constituents. For example, limestone, which is a soft rock, comes in white, yellow, cream, blue, gray, black, red, green, and varied colors like marble. Yellow or cream is an indication that it contains iron oxide, green that it contains chlorite, et cetera. Some rock, like quartz, is a very hard mineral. Limestone, on the other hand, when pure, may be readily scratched with a coin.

Thus far we have spoken mainly of phosphate rock, of which there are big deposits in Tennessee, Florida, and the Far West. But large amounts of granite rock are now being used for their potash content, some of these rocks containing as much as 12 per cent of this element. I know of a huge agricultural project of about three thousand acres in Florida where beans are grown. Recently they changed over from chemical fertilizer potash to granite dust and enjoyed the same yield they always had but saved an enormous sum of money.

Basalt Rock

Several years ago I went to Germany and stumbled upon a significant piece of information which, it seems to me, has great possibilities for the improvement of the organic method. At the Institute of Bio-dynamic Research in the town of Griesheim, I saw a few years' work in making compost with ground-up basalt rock which startled me. By using the basalt, mixed with clay, they were able to prevent the temperature of the heap from going above 120 degrees Fahrenheit. Regularly made compost will rise to 170 degrees—a tremendous difference— which gives sufficient heat to kill off bacteria and enzymes and to destroy valuable nutrients, especially nitrogen. It was astonishing to see many compost heaps in two rows, all of those in one row being made with basalt powder and those in the other row without any, the ones without the basalt having been "burned down" to a much lower height than the basalt ones. It was a sight for sore eyes. By the prevention of heating there

was very little dropping or compacting of the organic materials in the basalt heaps, but the decay was just as effective. In fact, the German government research men who visited this Institute were astonished at the darkness and quality of this basaltic compost. The basalt heaps also permitted the earthworms to work in them and to multiply, because of the lessened heat, and perhaps also because of the minerals in the basalt on which they thrived. There were thousands of them in each basalt heap, but relatively few in the other ones.

Dr. Hans Heinz and Kurt Willmann at the Institute spoke glowingly of the basalt-added compost as preserving nutrients and said that the high heat attained in the regular compost heaps caused tremendous losses of valuable plant food.

There are some basalts that have about one per cent of phosphate, but they are full of other minerals. It is a kind of rock that sometimes cleaves in practically straight lines, like shale or slate, and if you strike a blow upon it with a special kind of hammer, it will break. That is why some basalt rocks are used in making Belgian blocks, or cobblestones. In fact, the people at Griesheim secured their basalt powder at a quarry near by which makes cobblestones and where large heaps of powder which result as a by-product have accumulated. Anyone who wants it pays only twenty-five cents a ton for this residue material.

Basalt rock is widely distributed in the United States, the New England coast being especially seamed with deposits. It is found in the Adirondack and White mountains and in the Highlands of New York and New Jersey, at Mts. Tom and Holyoke, Mass., East and West Rock near New Haven, Conn., the Palisades on the Hudson, and many dikes in the Richmond, Va., and Deep River, N. C., coal fields. Around Lake Superior, both in the iron and in the copper regions, are still greater sheets, for many thousands of feet of basalt (diabase) are present on Keweenaw Point. On the north shore near Port Arthur, the headlands of Thunder Bay exhibit superb examples. The iron-bearing strata are penetrated by innumerable dikes. The greatest of all the American basaltic areas is, however, met in the Snake River region of southern Idaho and extends into eastern Oregon and Washington. Many thousands of square miles are covered with the dark lava and are locally called the "Lava Beds." In Colorado, as at the Table Mountains, near Golden and Fisher's Peak, near Trinidad, there are prominent sheets, and the same is true of many other points in this state. In New Mexico, Arizona, and Texas they are also met.

I wrote regarding basalt to Dr. W. D. Keller, professor of geology at the University of Missouri, and in his reply he stated, "Basalt rock is about the best-balanced rock I know of for supplying plant nutrients. Therefore, I believe that powdered basalt with an illite rich clay mixed with organic matter should provide the best average all-purpose plant food possible unless one would want to sweeten it up with a little extra phosphate rock." This jibes with the statement given me by Dr. Hans Heinz, of the Institute of Bio-dynamic Research, to the effect that the most fertile soils in Germany are those that have formed from an underlayer of basalt rock. In my opinion a mixture of phosphate, potash, and basalt rock powder would make the ideal mineral fertilizer, being well balanced in phosphate, potash, and the other needed mineral elements. The nitrogen would come from organic matter.

Basalt Powder Method of Composting in Germany

In making compost at Griesheim they first mix the basalt powder with clay, fifty-fifty, this mixture then representing 30 per cent of the total by weight of the heap. This seemed to me to be a large percentage of rock and clay, and I wondered whether this fact alone was responsible for the depression of the temperature. I decided to bear this in mind for future experimenting that we would do on our own farm. At Griesheim they stated that the basalt powder must not be too fine or it would cake into cement.

I admired the place they had chosen for making their compost—a grove of trees which permitted only a small amount of sun to reach the heaps. Too much sun or too little would be bad from a perfectionist's viewpoint. At Griesheim they found that on one side of compost heaps which did not get any sun at all the material became like peat, and it was not because of the lack of light but because of the absence of direct contact with radiations from the sun.

To protect the heaps in the early stages, before turning, they covered them neatly, top and sides, with one half inch of soil, plus, on top of that, about an inch of oak bark. In the absence of the latter they would use peat. This protected the mass from the drying action of the wind and sun. Of course they saw to it that the material was wetted down sufficiently as it was assembled, and they turned the heaps once or twice. The compost was of a wonderful quality. We were able to form it into compacted balls and then to break it up easily with the hand, a sure sign that it had decomposed nicely.

The basalt is also applied directly to the soil, as one would do with phosphate or potash rock. They have found at Griesheim that the basalt, if left on the surface, increases the temperature of the soil, but if worked in, it temporarily reduces it. Their practice is to leave the basalt powder on the surface of the soil one year and plow it in the next season. They claim that the basalt soon forms into clay, thus indicating that its nutrients are quickly available to growing crops. This would be a good amendment to apply to fruit orchards and direct to gardening soils.

Slate Residues as Fertilizer

I was told that in another part of Germany one of their associates had been very successful in using residues of slate as a fertilizer. Geologically the slates are very close to basalt but have somewhat higher contents of potash. They claim that if soft slate residues are used, not the kind used for roofs, it will break down into soil in only a year or two. This looks very exciting, because in many coal-mining regions there are tremendous piles of slate which have been separated from the coal and which can be had free for the hauling. Gardening clubs located in such regions would find this an excellent project for beautifying their communities and at the same time helping agriculture.

At this time let me report what I was told as a comparison between basalt and slate. Basalt was formed in a fire process (igneous), and in growing plants it aids in the seed-forming process. Slate, which was not formed by high heat, they believe, is good for the leaf-forming process.

I found that the earthworm and basalt were friends, and would suggest that those who are raising earthworms put a liberal sprinkling of basalt in their boxes and heaps. This means that less conditioning, or decaying of the organic matter, would be necessary before it is put in the boxes, as there will be less heating. At Griesheim they transfer earthworms from heap to heap as new ones are made, because of the large quantities which result from conditions favorable to their multiplication.

A few weeks after my return from Germany, J. A. Johnson of Organic Gardens, Fullerton, Maryland, visited me, and when I told him about the ability of basalt to reduce temperature, he told me that he was using this rock powder in his new soil conditioner called *Soil-till,* which he developed as his answer to

Krilium. He also mentioned that in compost heaps where he had used liberal amounts of basic slag the temperatures were significantly depressed. Basic slag is a phosphate-containing by-product of the Bessemer steelmaking process, a material which has been subjected to extremely high temperatures. We immediately set up an experiment in composting with basic slag and we found that Mr. Johnson was right. Immediately after the first day the basic slag heap was a few degrees lower in temperature than the other, and after about ten days the slag heap was about 108 degrees Fahrenheit while the regular one was about 130 degrees. We are now setting up heaps made of basalt, granite rock, phosphate rock, et cetera, and would suggest that some of our readers may like to do the same. If they do, we would certainly like to hear from them.

In making a compost heap consisting of about six tons of matter, almost one ton would be phosphate rock. If the six tons are applied to one acre, the one ton of phosphate would not be too much. Besides, the effect of the decaying organic matter would make the phosphate more available.

This subject must be investigated thoroughly. The U. S. Department of Agriculture is the logical one to do it, because it could save American farmers billions of dollars. Thousands of cattle are dying of hoof-and-mouth disease every year, probably because the soil in which their food grows lacks trace minerals. The situation has become so alarming that an international conference of agriculturists has been called. The cure and the prevention may be as simple as putting ground-up rocks of various kinds in the soil. Our wealth of rock is unlimited. Here is a new science in the making. The rock quarry owners ought to become excited about it, for it means great increases in income for them and removal of unsightly defacements from the landscape.

SEVENTEEN

POISON SPRAYS

Something sinister is occurring in American agricultural practice—far worse, in my opinion, than anything the imagination of agronomical science has conceived thus far—which should be a cause for great alarm. It concerns a new method of preventing insect infestation in plants by means of poisonous insecticides, and involves such a dangerous mode of action that I wonder if, in adopting it, financially hungry industry isn't going a bit too far.

About seventy-five years ago the poison spraying of apple trees was practically an unknown procedure in orcharding. Some insects came to plague the apples, but Nature provided enemy insects which kept the troublemakers in check. But, as is always the case with Nature, it was not a 100-per-cent effective arrangement and some fruit damage occurred. The public was used to seeing and even eating an apple here and there that exhibited an insect bite or two. However, a trend was developing in American life which demanded perfection of appearance. It was part of the movement that gave America automobiles with beautiful chromium fittings. The public began to demand white eggs, thinking they were "purer," and willingly paid a premium for them. Apples had to be large and perfect, without an insect bite or other disfiguring blemish. The citrus interests began to add color to oranges, and the dairy people put the cancer-causing butter yellow (now banned) into butter. Industry scandalously pandered to the consumer's taste for beauty and added eye appeal to all items of food regardless of how it damaged their nutritional values.

As the years went on, the problems in the orchards became more perplexing. The chemist mastered one insect and another appeared from nowhere. In one season chemical X destroyed insect Y, but the next year insect Y developed a tolerance to poison X. This led to the perfection of more and more powerful chemical compounds and the need for increasing the number of applications to about fifteen or sixteen a season, disturbing the balance of Nature to such an extent that even the bees that were needed by the orchardist to pollinate the apple blossoms disappeared, so that the farmer had to hire additional people to hand-pollinate his trees. And when this insecticidal bludgeoning with poison sprays got beyond the physical capability of the farmer to handle, he took to the air, and in 1951 the farmers of the United States used six thousand five hundred airplanes to shower upon the earth these expensive chemical poisons.

Entomologists' Attitude

The entomologists—those people who spend their lives trying to prove that man is superior to the insect—are having a tough time. They are frantically attempting to breed varieties of fruits and vegetables that are more resistant to disease and insects.

They are working feverishly to discover magic formulas that will stop the insect dead in its tracks. But for a long time they have had a dangerous idea in the back of their heads. Why not, they say, feed some kind of poison to the plant instead of to the insect, so that every cell and bit of tissue becomes saturated with it? Thus when an insect feeds upon the plant it will be done for. This would be science with a vengeance. They thought of it for so long that they actually did it.

Early in 1952 such a product was launched with powerful hullabaloo. Made from coal, it has the chemical name of Octamethyl Pyrophosphoramide and is either put on the soil around the roots or is sprayed onto the plant itself. In either case it forces itself into every cell of the entire plant. One can judge the potency of such a chemical which has the power of forcing itself so thoroughly and saturating every part of a plant.

Several years ago this idea was discussed in agricultural literature and it was announced that soon such a product would be placed on the market. When I was called as a witness, a few years ago, in a hearing in Washington conducted by the Pure Food and Drug Administration for the purpose of determining permissible residues of poison sprays on foods, I expressed alarm at the possibility that such a practice might be encouraged on food crops, that the public would be eating foods every cell of which was tainted by these systemic chemicals. Up jumped a representative of one of the insecticide companies and stated that it was not the intention that this product be used on food crops. It was only thought of for ornamental plants. But in my mind I harbored misgivings. It was a dangerous trend. I was sure that it was bound eventually to be used on edible crops, and that is exactly what is happening.

Professor R. W. Leiby, entomologist of Cornell University, in the June 1952 *Country Gentleman,* speaks of experiments with Systox on potatoes and apples, and states, "Much more experimentation must be made with the systemic insecticides before they will be approved for use on fruits, vegetables, or crops fed to livestock."

Systemic Spray Complications

The U. S. Department of Agriculture, at the time this spray was announced, advised that the systemic types of insect poisons were definitely not for use on edible crops, although it did state that someday it might be recommended for such crops. If that day ever comes, it will be the most formidable blow ever struck against the interest and the health of our citizenry. It will be the biggest step yet taken toward race suicide through the sterilization of the reproductive functions of man by the irritating effect upon them of these harmful systemic chemicals.

The experts say that systemic insecticides do not remain long inside a plant and that if you wait a few weeks after fruit and vegetables have been treated, they will be safe to eat. But in the same breath they state that the systemic insecticides last three to four times longer than ordinary poisons. I have seen so many of these sales-talk statements proven to be false that I do not trust this one. I do not think that all of the poison will be excreted by the plant, and if it does, what effect will it produce on the plant's tissue while it is contained within it? And who is going to fence in all the orchards and farms to keep innocent wayfarers from this deadly produce before the poison is excreted?

Economic Aspects vs. Health Aspects

One newspaper states that this type of spray will save the nation's farmers millions of dollars' worth of crops a year; but,

I might add, it could cause the people who eat foods raised by its aid tens of millions of dollars in medical and hospital costs. Business is in the form of a monetary equation, and we must not fail to study that formula in its every aspect, paying attention to both sides. The agricultural press wildly acclaims a new product, mouthing the prepared statements of the manufacturers to the effect that the product is not dangerous to human beings in the quantity present in the harvested crop. But if it is added to all the food preservatives, all the germ killers, the benzoates of soda, the chlorine and alum in water, the sodium nitrite in frankfurters, the chemicals in bread and in every item of food on the daily menu, what then would be the total cumulative effect? I am sure such a test has not been made.

This is a situation that calls for immediate action. The public must speak out boldly and at once. It must write to congressmen, senators, newspapers, agricultural colleges, and the Pure Food and Drug Administration, asking that an unqualified ban be placed on this type of insecticide, even for ornamental plants, because there are too many uneducated farmers and truck gardeners who will be tempted to use it on food crops if they can purchase it for ornamental use. This subject must be brought up for discussion in public forums and at parent-teacher meetings. The public has an inalienable right to eat unpoisoned food, and industry must learn to make profits without infringing upon that right.

After reading about the systemic type of poison spray, the ordinary kind that is sprayed on the outside of a plant seems almost innocuous. But an organic gardener never uses them, for several reasons. First, they remain on vegetables and even penetrate under skins, being a danger to the health of those who consume them. Secondly, they fall upon the earth and contaminate the soil and the micro-organisms that work in it.

In time the ability of such a soil to produce a crop is seriously affected. The point is that organic gardeners have found that they get more than satisfactory crops without spraying.

Here and there trouble is encountered. I have never been able to control the Mexican bean beetle, but although it makes a few holes in the leaves, I have never noticed any effect on the bean pods. These it does not touch. A few flea beetles may get out of hand sometimes, but by and large the average organically run garden is a wonderful sight for the eyes without benefit of poison-spray can.

This subject may be divided into two parts—disease and insect infestation. With regard to the first there is extremely little trouble. According to the experts—for instance, Dr. Waksman of Rutgers College—the mere presence of organic matter in the soil acts as a controlling agent, an inhibitor of plant disease. But how it does this is open to discussion. Perhaps it multiplies the antibiotic organisms which maintain law and order in the soil. However it does so, the inspection of the average organic garden will reveal that the plants are clean and practically free of disease.

Resistance to Disease

Everyone harbors disease organisms. It is said that every person carries around tuberculosis germs. If the body remains strong and healthy, the disease germs cannot act up, they remain inactive. But let the body weaken in some respect and the germs cause trouble. It could be the same with a plant. The health of organically grown plants can be seen from the roots up. They are in the pink. The bad actors of the disease world cannot do much with them.

In an experiment at the Connecticut Agricultural Experiment Station (Bulletin 500, November 1946) in the control of fusarium root rot in squash, it was found that the application of organic matter to the soil where diseased squash seed were planted resulted in the growing of healthy plants, absolutely free of this disease. There are dozens of similar instances in scientific literature. Just one season of growing plants by the organic method will convince you of the truth of these statements.

In regard to the insect it is a much more difficult problem. But there seems to be some evidence that the insect is attracted to plants that are diseased, weakened, that contain imbalances of mineral make-up; that possibly the insect is a censor of Nature, evolved over millions of years as Nature's tool to destroy unwanted vegetation. The insect on occasion prefers a plant with a high carbohydrate content, and it is known that the overuse of potash in chemical fertilizers causes an oversupply of carbohydrates to form in a plant. In my own gardening I have seen the working out of this principle. But there are many exceptions. Not every insect knows or follows all of Nature's rules set down for him.

However, the last thing in the world I would do would be to douse all my plants with poison, especially the vegetables that I intend to eat. If necessary, I would grow a little more. I would share: I would grow some for the insect and some for me. But I do not want to have any poison sprays around the place. There is a health hazard to the gardener in the very act of spraying them.

In connection with commercial orcharding and truck farming, the question of the insect will have to be given some further study. But as for the home gardener, he can put plenty of organic matter in the soil, use rock powders instead of chemical fertilizers, and never use poison sprays. They are a waste of money and time.

EIGHTEEN

DISEASE, INSECTS, AND NATURAL METHODS OF CONTROL

A plant disease may be defined as any abnormality in a plant produced by some causative agent. The causative agent may be a bacterium, a fungus, or other parasitic organism; or it may be some unfavorable environmental condition as, for instance, a deficiency of one or more of the elements which are necessary for the normal growth and development of plants.

A living organism which causes a disease in plants is usually referred to as a *pathogene*. Pathogenes belong to the groups of bacteria, fungi, viruses, slime molds, and some animals, such as nematodes. Some of these, like the powdery mildews, are external parasites but send absorbing organs into the tissues of the plant on which they live. The plant from which a parasite takes its food is known as its *host*. Some parasites live on a single host, like grape mildew, while others live on two or more different kinds of host plants, like the wheat-rust fungus which lives alternately on wheat and the American barberry.

The successful establishment of a parasite on its host is called *infection*. The infection of plants of a garden or field from an outside source is known as *primary infection*. The spreading of the disease from one plant to another in the same garden is known as *secondary infection*. Many diseases can be controlled by preventing secondary infection. This can be done by eliminating all diseased plants as a result of primary infection.

Most plant diseases are caused by parasitic fungi. Effective control involves the creation of conditions in plants which will be unfavorable to the growth of these parasitic fungi. Plants which are nutritionally well balanced are, as a rule, healthy and relatively free from the common plant diseases. To have such plants in the garden consideration must be given to (1) well-adapted varieties, (2) a well-prepared soil rich in humus and the essential elements, and (3) cultural practices.

Plants are covered with an effective, often disease-resistant epidermis. It is only after the epidermis has been broken that disease-producing fungi and bacteria can gain an entrance into the plant. Even slight damage is sufficient to make a plant vulnerable to these fungi, as brushing against and breaking off a few epidermal hairs of a squash leaf. Who knows how many diseased plants are the result of slight injuries to plants in the cultivating and hoeing processes? Such injuries not only provide an entrance for disease-producing organisms but lower the vitality of the plant to the point where it cannot resist the parasite.

Signs and Symptoms of Diseases Produced by Pathogenes

Every part of a plant—root, stem, leaf, flower, fruit, bark, wood, seed—is subject to disease, and the same disease may manifest itself in many or all parts of the plant body. Those marks or evidences which indicate a diseased condition in a plant are known as the *signs* and *symptoms* of the disease. The most common signs of disease are (1) a dying of the tissue (necrosis), resulting in such conditions as rot, canker, blight, wilt, damping-off, spot, streak, burn, and shot hole; (2) an overgrowth of tissues (hyperplasia), resulting in such abnormal growths as witches'-broom, galls, hairy root, curl, and scab; and (3) an undergrowth of tissues to produce such conditions as dwarfing and chlorosis (incomplete development of the leaf pigments).

Signs of Nutritional Diseases

Abnormalities in plants caused by the deficiency of one or more of the essential elements are sometimes referred to as *hunger signs*. It is difficult to determine whether the symptoms produced as a result of the shortage of a given element come about because the element is required for certain life processes or because it antagonizes some other element. A deficiency of one element generally implies excesses of other elements. Such deficiencies may be brought about by adding to the soil liberal amounts of highly soluble chemical fertilizers. Plants are much slower to manifest deficiency effects when an element is removed from the soil than they are in assuming a normal healthy condition when the element is restored to a deficient soil. Visual symptoms of nutrient deficiency may appear in all organs, including leaves, stems, roots, flowers, fruits, and seeds.

Deficiency symptoms of the more important nutrient elements are somewhat as follows:

NITROGEN. A nitrogen deficiency expresses itself in grasses by a yellowish-green color in the leaves, followed by drying of older leaves.

PHOSPHORUS. Deficiencies of phosphorus are expressed

somewhat differently in different plants. In corn and small grains the leaves assume purplish tints, legumes become bluish green and are stunted in growth, while in most plants the leaves become dark green with a tendency to develop reddish and purple colors.

POTASSIUM. A deficiency of potassium manifests itself by a yellowing of the leaves in the form of streaking or mottling of the older leaves, with a tendency of such parts of the leaves to die.

MAGNESIUM. The most common symptoms of deficiency include a yellowing, dying, bronzing, and reddening of the older leaves, commonly followed by a shedding of the leaves.

SULPHUR. A sulphur deficiency is indicated by the yellowing of the younger leaves in the initial stages of the deficiency and finally by yellowing of all the leaves. The yellowing of leaves is commonly referred to as *chlorosis*.

IRON. Iron deficiency is revealed by the chlorosis of the new leaves at the growing tips of the plant.

MANGANESE. The deficiency of manganese is revealed by the chlorosis of the young leaves, as in iron deficiency, followed by an early death of the leaves. Most deficiencies occur in neutral or alkaline soils.

COPPER. The principal symptom of copper deficiency is withertip, in which the leaves at the stem tip wilt and do not recover overnight or during cloudy weather.

ZINC. Zinc deficiency is revealed in a variety of ways, as yellowing between the veins followed by the dying of the tissue in tobacco, little leaf in pecans and citrus trees, and leaf spot in sugar beet and potato.

BORON. A common symptom of boron deficiency is the dying of the growing tip of plant stems, internal cork in apples, water-soaked areas and bitter taste of cauliflower, and cracked leaf stalk in celery.

Prevention of Plant Diseases

In plant diseases, as in so many other matters, an ounce of prevention is worth a pound of cure.

Sanitation is of the utmost importance in the prevention of plant diseases. Diseased plant parts, including stems, leaves, and fruits, should be put in the compost heap to be converted into compost.

Crop rotation has been advised for the prevention and control of many plant diseases. If the same kinds of plants are grown in the same soil year after year, parasites are likely to accumulate to the point which makes growing this kind of plant unprofitable.

A living soil, one rich in soil organisms, is usually one having a high organic-matter content and all the nutrient elements in good balance. Such a soil is the best kind of insurance against plant diseases. Tillage of the soil also is an important factor in the control of plant diseases, as it provides conditions favorable to a vigorous growth. Waksman and others have recently shown that in artificial media different bacteria and fungi manufacture substances of varying degrees of antibiotic activity to other bacteria and fungi. It is possible that antibiotics are produced in living soils which keep crop plants free from disease. It is a common observation in pot experiments that certain diseases, such as the root rots of cereals, are more destructive in steri-lized soil than in comparable non-sterilized soil, both being equally inoculated with the pathogens. In such experiments, if bits of the original soil are introduced into the sterilized soil, the microflora is quickly re-established, the pathogene checked, and the disease controlled.

The physical condition of the soil has an important bearing on the prevention and control of diseases. Important are such factors as temperature, aeration, moisture, and soil reaction. Some disease-producing organisms attack their host plants in soils of certain temperatures, but not when soils have a different and, apparently for the pathogene, unfavorable temperature. For instance, yellows in crucifers caused by *Fusarium conglu-tinans* occurs in soils with a higher temperature but does not show up when the crucifers are grown in cooler soils. An entire tomato crop may be destroyed by wilt caused by Verticillium in wet soil, while the plants will be entirely immune when grown in a well-drained soil. It has long been recognized that potato scab is less prevalent in soils that have a reaction below 5.2 than in soils with a higher pH value. The pH value becomes less important as the humus content of the soil increases; the humus acts as an effective buffer in the soil. The physical factors of the soil and air are so interrelated when it comes to their possible effects on pathogenes that it is not easy to say just what effect each has separately.

Control of Some Common Plant Diseases

The actual occurrence of a plant disease is a sure sign that one or more requirements of the plant for normal health and growth has not been met completely. The trouble, as a rule, is in the soil and can be corrected. Sometimes the difficulty is in the atmosphere, such as a prolonged period of inclement weather.

ASPARAGUS RUST. Remove all badly infested plants to the compost heap, where they will be included in the compost to be used later to fertilize the asparagus bed.

BEAN RUST. Include all diseased plants in the compost heap to be used later in fertilizing the bean rows. Be careful to plant varieties of beans resistant to the rust.

POWDERY MILDEWS. Remove infected plants as soon as they can be recognized and remove them to the compost heap. Mildews can be largely prevented by properly enriching the soil in humus.

POTATO SCAB. This is a common disease of the potato and can be inhibited to a large extent by keeping the soil reaction low, say at a pH of 5.2. It has been shown by Hugh Ward (*Organic Farmer*, August 1949, page 15) that potato scab will not develop in soil sufficiently rich in humus, even with a pH as high as 7.2 to 7.5.

EARLY BLIGHT OF POTATO. Vigorous plants are said to withstand the attack, so that a soil that will insure rapid, healthy growth is the key to this disease.

LATE BLIGHT OF POTATO. This blight, like so many other blights, can be largely prevented by keeping the soil in good heart. The most important factor is a high humus content.

TOMATO BLIGHT. Same as late blight of potato.

DOWNY MILDEWS. Downy mildews occur on many food plants as a result of unfavorable growth conditions. If any plant shows downy mildew, it should be removed immediately to the compost heap.

BLACK ROT OF CABBAGE. Remove infected leaves as detected, and practice sanitation in every way possible.

RUST OF WHEAT. Eliminate the American barberry.

RUST OF APPLE. Eliminate red-cedar trees, which are the alternate host of this rust-producing fungus.

BROWN ROT OF STONE FRUITS. Remove all fruit mummies from the tree and ground and all dead leaves from beneath the trees. Band the trees to prevent crawling insects from climbing them.

WITCHES'-BROOM. Remove the brooms to the compost heap.

A sufficient number of examples have been given to indicate the use of natural methods for preventing or controlling plant diseases. The occurrence of a disease should be regarded as an indication of a mistake in cultural practices rather than as a sign that poisonous sprays should be used. By studying the situation carefully, an intelligent gardener can usually learn the cause of the disease, not in terms of a pathogene but rather in terms of cultural practice.

Planting Resistant Varieties

Some varieties of plants seem to be much more resistant to pathogenes than others. Seeds taken from plants grown in your own garden are apt to be better adapted to your conditions than seeds grown elsewhere, especially if they have been grown and selected over a number of years.

Since many garden plants are natives of other countries, it is important to become familiar with the environmental conditions of their native lands. Plants of the desert and open meadow require lots of light, while plants of the woodland prefer some shade.

For each kind of plant, learn whether it prefers an acid or slightly alkaline soil, a northern or southern exposure, a heavy or light soil, a well-drained or wet soil, a long or short day, a dry or humid atmosphere.

A garden planted to one kind of vegetable and a field planted to one kind of crop represent monoculture, a practice which usually is avoided by Nature. Out of cultivation, plants grow in mixed cultures—that is, many species of plants grow together to form a more or less complex plant society. Our grandmothers' gardens contained vegetables, flowers, herbs, and small fruits, and for this reason, perhaps, were damaged less by pests than present-day vegetable gardens in which are grown only a few kinds of plants and no flowers and herbs.

Insects

Very little study has been devoted to *non-poisonous* means of controlling insects, but there is evidence that if the entomologists fifty years ago had started with this in mind, the farmer and gardener would not only have the situation in control but the cost would be very low. As it is, orcharding today is becoming more and more unprofitable due to the high cost of spray poisons. In England, however, there is not half the number of poison sprays used on farms per season as in the United States. This is because the farmer has always maintained the organic-matter content of his soil by having sufficient cattle and by using long rotations, a large part of which are pasture grasses. As a result, at the end of three or four years there is a large quantity of matter to plow under.

Much of the trouble we have with insects can be avoided if we follow Nature's methods in our gardening. The more we observe her methods, the more we come to understand that the insect is Nature's censor in destroying unwanted vegetation. If a plant is growing on the wrong kind of soil, the leaves may take on an off-taste. This, as well as its appearance, is recognizable by insects. There seems to be evidence that many insects prefer to feed upon plant matter that has imbalances in its chemical make-up or plant matter which is mildly diseased. Do insects prefer such food? It seems that Nature has provided them to remove the unfit. Insects are not merely an accident. They are part of a scheme of evolution wherein they serve important functions.

I had an experience with two grapevines growing next to each other which gave me an inkling that there was method in this insect behavior. One of these vines was a very old one. We planted a new one near it and soon observed that the Japanese beetles were present only on the leaves of the old one, even though the leaves of the two vines intermingled. The old vine was in its old age—tired and unresponsive to the nutrition we were giving it. The leaf tissue was subnormal in some respect, and the Japanese beetle preferred it.

Here is another experience. In our hothouse we grew some lettuce in December, but the plants were attacked by aphids (plant lice). In February, on the very same spot and without fumigating, we planted another crop of lettuce which did not harbor a single aphid. This made me think. In December the days were short and there had been little sun. The lettuce was stunted. In February the days were much longer and there was good sun. The aphids came to destroy the stunted lettuce, since one of their functions is that of scavenger. Last winter we planted in our hothouse some kohlrabi plants which had been grown from seed in flats. We had much trouble with slugs that practically destroyed the whole crop. It was evident that the shock of the transplanting weakened them, causing a peculiar taste to the plants, which was to the slugs' liking. We then planted kohlrabi seed directly in the soil, where it grew to maturity, and there was no more trouble with slugs.

I could cite a dozen other similar instances. I can also tell you from personal experience and from researches that exist in scientific gardening literature that, in general, insects prefer to feed on plants grown with chemical fertilizers rather than on those grown by the organic method. We must, however, also be careful that we do not violate other rules of Nature.

General Instructions

Control of insect pests is possible in any number of ways, without resorting to the use of poison sprays and chemicals. Plants strongly attacked by insects are often nutritionally unbalanced. Be sure that you give them a completely fertile soil, rich in organic matter and all the minerals. Using a good-sized mulch and making compost will help, as well as adding minerals in the form of natural rock fertilizers.

Predators in Pest Control

An animal which devours another animal for food is called a *predator*. Important insect predators in the garden are the ladybird beetle, ichneumon fly, praying mantis, and lacewing.

Toads are especially valuable in the control of garden pests. Pests can be controlled on the low-growing plants by inducing toads to become garden residents. Toads will continue their residence only as long as there is a sufficient food supply. They will not take dead or motionless food. Their food consists of cutworms, tent caterpillars, ants, myriapods, spiders, sow bugs, snails, worms, grasshoppers, some beetles, and various other insects.

It has been estimated that about two thirds of the food of birds consists of insects. The food varies greatly with the season, depending largely upon availability. Most birds feed freely on insects during the summer months, but in fall, winter, and early spring they feed on various fruits and seeds. Woodpeckers and nuthatches, however, are forever examining the trunks and branches of trees for insects in hiding.

Prevention and Sanitation

What is true of plant disease is true of garden pests—an ounce of prevention is worth a pound of cure. Insects are cold-blooded creatures. Early in the morning they are apt to be slow and sluggish, but during the warm part of the day they are alert and fleet. Bean beetles, for instance, spend the winter as adults in some sheltered place. Only a very small per cent pass the winter successfully and appear on the bean plants in spring. These few, obligingly enough, feed on the upper surface of the leaves, where they can be apprehended and caught. By hand-picking the few adults which do appear, an epidemic of beetles on the beans can be prevented.

Hand-picking is an effective preventive measure for all insects large enough to pick, such as potato beetles, cucumber beetles, tomato worms, Japanese beetles, and cutworms. A suitable band or girdle to prevent ants and other crawling insects from establishing aphids and other pests on the leaves of trees may be made as follows. First put a girdle of cotton around the trunk. Over the cotton place a girdle or band of roofing paper, which can be secured by the use of small box nails. Then, with a brush, apply tree tanglefoot over the band of roofing. The tanglefoot may have to be renewed from time to time to prevent crawling insects from crossing over the girdle on the dead bodies of those which tried to cross the girdle before them.

Very small insects—such as aphids, flea beetles, and red spiders—can be washed off the plants with a stream of water from a pressure tank or ordinary sprayer. As a rule, aphids and spiders washed off a plant do not return. Washing them off early, or washing the plants before they appear or become apparent, is an effective method of prevention.

Harmless Spray Mixture

A relatively harmless 3-per-cent-oil spray could be applied to trees, but only while the trees are dormant. This need not be resorted to unless the insect infestation is extremely serious.

Some Common Garden Pests and How to Control Them

ANTS. We do not recommend the use of Cyanogas for exterminating ants, as this will ruin your soil. When you get your land rich organically, you will find that the ant problem will take care of itself. Organic matter in the soil increases its moisture content and makes conditions less favorable for the ants. Actually, ants are really beneficial in the compost heap and in the soil, as they increase aeration. They seldom injure plants. While they sometimes carry aphids from one plant to another, this can be prevented by banding the plants and trees with some suitable non-poisonous material.

APHIDS. Aphids may be controlled by first practicing sanitary measures. Do not crowd plants so that they are not well exposed to sunlight and air. Then use plenty of compost in growing plants that are susceptible to aphids. In most cases bad infestations of aphids can be prevented by watching the plants closely and removing infested leaves and putting them in the compost heap

BAGWORMS. If only a few shrubs or small trees are to be considered in the control of bagworms, hand-picking and destruction of the cocoons during the winter months will be all that is required to prevent damage during the following season. The young caterpillars migrate with great difficulty and will not reinfect any tree to a serious extent in one season.

BEAN WEEVIL. Bean weevils attack the matured seeds of beans after they are harvested and put into storage if they have not been properly cured. This can be prevented by curing the beans before they are shelled and stored. When the beans are ready to be harvested, pull up the plants with the pods on them and put them on stakes to hold them off the ground to cure. The curing process involves certain biological changes, including fermentations and the production of heat; this requires six weeks or longer. The cured beans may then be shelled and stored in a dry place without danger of weevil damage.

CABBAGE BUTTERFLY. It is said that cabbage butterflies are repelled when such odorous plants as hemp, nasturtium, and tomato and such aromatic plants as catnip, rosemary, and sage are planted near or among the cabbage plants. To control the cabbage worm, which is the larvae of the butterfly, try trapping it with a blue lamp used during the daylight. The worms will be attracted from long distances.

CABBAGE MAGGOT. This insect can be prevented from infecting cabbage plants by placing a cardboard disk around the plant at planting time. Or seedlings and young plants can be grown in flats that are screened to prevent approach of the adult flies. Another important control measure consists in setting the plants out at a time when the flies are not on wing.

The cabbage maggot can be largely avoided by sowing the seed and growing the seedlings either before or after the adults of this insect are on wing.

CATERPILLARS. Small caterpillars can best be controlled by the encouragement and protection of native birds which eat caterpillars. Protect the birds from cats and other enemies, and provide birdhouses in which they may rear their young.

CENTIPEDES. Centipedes must be classed as beneficial organisms. They feed on insects, worms, mollusks, and other small animals, many of which are injurious to plants. They destroy many injurious insects, slugs, and perhaps a few earthworms. In a different way they are as beneficial as earthworms. Protect them rather than harm them.

CHINCH BUG. Professor Leonard Haseman of the University of Missouri has found that when the chinch bug is fed on plants grown in nitrogen-poor soil, it not only lives longer but lays more eggs. Haseman feels that well-fed crops will give better insect control.

Soybeans growing as a companion crop with corn shade the bases of the corn plants so that they will be avoided by the highly destructive chinch bugs.

CODLING MOTH. Traps baited with sassafras oil are a good control for the codling moth. A solid bait for codling moth may be made by filling a small ice-cream cup two thirds full of sawdust, stirring into the sawdust a teaspoonful of sassafrass oil and a tablespoonful of glacial acetic acid, and then adding enough liquid glue to saturate the sawdust mixture thoroughly. When the cup is dry, after a day or two, suspend it in a mason jar partly filled with water.

CORN BORER. The most effective and simplest method of controlling the corn borer consists of removing the cornstalks cut off at the ground level as soon as the crop has matured and is harvested. Daylight-blue lamps will also capture the corn borer.

CORN-EAR WORM. The variety Erie is resistant to the corn-ear worm.

CORN WEEVIL. Florida W–1, Whatley, and Georgia 103 are resistant varieties.

CUCUMBER BEETLE. A recommended method of control consists of mixing a handful of wood ashes and a handful of hydrated lime in two gallons of water and spraying both under and upper sides of the leaves. This treatment does not kill the beetles but does seem to drive them away.

CUTWORMS. Cutworms chew plants off more or less completely at the ground level. They do this damage to plants at night, and usually hide beneath soil or other shelter during the day. A simple device for preventing damage to plants is to place a paper collar around the stem extending for some distance above and below the ground level.

Cutworms are becoming more and more plentiful because toads and other insect-eating animals are becoming increasingly scarce. These cutworm-destroying animals are killed by eating poisoned insects. Some gardeners keep a half-dozen bantams in the garden for keeping cutworms under control.

Daylight-blue lamps may also be used.

FLEA BEETLES. Flea beetles are extremely small and feed on the leaves of seedling plants. By planting the seed thick, and thinning after danger of flea-beetle damage is past, a cull row of vegetables can be grown. Thinning must be done before crowding prevents good circulation of air about the plants.

It is also possible to control flea beetles by using equal parts of old soot and agricultural lime, which emits an odor that repels the beetles. This mixture should be put in small containers rather than on the soil or on the plants.

Potato varieties resistant to flea beetles are Sequoia and Doe Bay Red.

GRASSHOPPERS. Grasshoppers can be caught by various baits laid out in the morning, but a sound non-chemical method consists of the use of buckets or tubs with water and a light placed near by. Thus one gets grasshoppers that can be fed to chickens. It is also advisable to encourage birds which eat these insects.

Grasshoppers lay their eggs in soil not covered with plants. Keeping a good ground cover goes a long way toward preventing egg laying in your soil.

HOUSEFLIES. Houseflies may best be controlled by the elimination of their breeding places. Devices for reducing their numbers are tanglefoot flypapers and electric fly killers. Do not spray with DDT, as this will lead only to the origin of a DDT-resistant strain, which is even worse than the regular flies.

JAPANESE BEETLES. The Japanese beetle was first discovered in this country in 1916. When and how it was introduced is unknown. It is a native of Japan, where it is not a serious pest because of the cultural practices used there and because of the presence of its natural enemies. It has become a serious pest in this country because its natural enemies are not here to keep it under control. Natural enemies are being introduced, however, and in time it will be brought into balance. Among the most important control organisms are the "milky disease" of the larvae and certain parasitic wasps.

On our organic gardening experimental farm the Japanese beetle has been successfully appeased by the growth of a non-food plant which it seems to prefer above all other plants—the *odorless* marigold. When this marigold was planted next to corn, the beetles did not chew off the corn silks. The beetles can also be caught by traps baited with geranium oil. Geranium plants, which, when eaten, will kill the beetles, may also be grown in the garden. A disease organism which is fatal to the Japanese-beetle larvae is called milky spore disease and may be purchased in seed stores. It is applied to the soil when the larvae winter.

LEAF MINERS. The leaf miner can be controlled fairly well by the practice of sanitation. Be sure that all waste plant materials and other objects under which these insects hide and hibernate during the winter are cleaned up and placed in the compost heap. One plant in particular which serves as a host for the leaf miner is lamb's-quarters (*Chenopodium album*).

The leaf miner should become less of a problem as your soil becomes richer in humus and in the essential nutrient elements. Such plants are lower in carbohydrates and less palatable to these insects.

MEALY BUGS. Mealy bugs may be cleaned off special plants with a cotton swab soaked in alcohol.

MEXICAN BEAN BEETLES. Hand-picking the adults which succeed in surviving the winter is the simplest and best method of keeping these insects under control. They have few natural enemies. Some ladybugs feed on the eggs and young larvae of the bean beetle. Ground beetles have been observed to feed on the larvae. One parasitic fly is known but has not yet been established in the new range of the insect.

MITES AND SPIDERS. Mites and spiders are usually best controlled by the maintenance of a proper balance of organisms. Do not use poison sprays, because usually they kill the enemies of mites and spiders but do not kill mites themselves. Under such circumstances, mites become a serious menace to our crop plants. We have many indications that plants grown with plenty of humus are relatively immune from damage from mites.

MOTHS. Moths may be trapped, but the traps must be in operation when a particular moth is on wing. Each kind of moth has a particular season when the adults are on wing and attack plants. Many kinds of moths are nocturnal in their habits.

As to the brown-tail moth, the winter webs may be collected by hand and destroyed. In the case of both bagworm and the brown-tail moth, rotenone may be used on non-food plants in extreme cases.

NEMATODES. Many cases have come to our attention where the consistent use of compost has eliminated nematodes. Sir Albert Howard described a case where nematodes were killed out merely by the application of humus. No chemicals should be used for their extermination, as this will interfere with the proper functioning of beneficial soil organisms which tend to keep all dangerous microbes and nematodes in check.

It has been found that a heavy mulch reduces root knot in plants by nematodes. When a crop of sweet clover is plowed under, the heat and gas from the decaying materials kill large numbers of nematodes, including cysts.

Varieties of lima beans showing high resistance include Rico 8402, Rico 1216, and 12M.

RADISH MAGGOT. In Wisconsin, Crimson Giant and Scarlet Globe radishes were found to be more resistant to maggot than Cavalier.

SCALES. Scales can be controlled by spraying trees and shrubs, *while in the dormant condition,* with a 3-per-cent-oil spray. This kills the scale insects by forming a film over their bodies which excludes oxygen needed by them in respiration. The oil is not poisonous and will do little damage to either plants or soil.

SLUGS. At least two species of garden slugs may become troublesome in the garden. The more common is the gray field slug; the other one is the giant or spotted garden slug. These animals hide under rubbish during the day and feed at night on tender leaves of many garden plants, leaving a slimy trail where they have crawled. Jellylike eggs are laid in the fall and spring in the soil or under stones, sticks, and clods of earth. Slugs may be trapped beneath shingles or other pieces of board and then killed. Plant and flower beds may be protected by sprinkling hydrated or air-slaked lime or wood ashes on the soil, as slugs and snails do not willingly crawl through dry materials. Proper garden sanitation, such as removing all rubbish and plant materials to the compost heap, will help to control slugs. Do not use poisonous chemicals. An inverted cabbage leaf also makes a good trap for snails and slugs.

SOWBUGS. The best way to rid your garden of sowbugs is to encourage toads and lizards. By constantly enriching your land with compost, eventually some reasonable equilibrium will be established by the processes of Nature. Sowbugs usually live in decaying organic matter and help to form humus. In the compost heap, sowbugs perform a noble service.

Sowbugs prefer a somewhat acid medium. One reader reported that when he made compost without lime he was visited by sowbugs, but when he used lime in the compost heap the sowbugs disappeared.

SQUASH BUGS. The squash bug can be discouraged by keeping the squash plants dusted with wood ashes. If applied early in the morning, when the leaves are wet with dew, the ashes will adhere to the leaf surfaces. Be sure to keep the leaves dusted until the plants are old enough to resist the squash bugs.

TOMATO WORM. The best method of control is hand-picking. If necessary, a daylight-blue lamp can be used.

WEBWORMS. Spray the trunks and branches of trees with a tree paste made of equal parts of fresh cow manure and clay sufficiently diluted in water to pass through a spray nozzle.

WIREWORMS. Wireworms live in acid soils which are not properly aerated. As a matter of fact, wireworms are good indicators that the soil has become acid through improper aeration. Wireworms often occur in great numbers in an old sod where they live on grass roots. The soil under the sod is poorly aerated and somewhat acid. The wireworms help to convert the plant roots into compost.

To control wireworms, aerate the soil and enrich it with compost. Soil organisms in the compost will bring the wireworm under control. It is poor practice to plant a cultivated crop in a field that has had sod on it for a long time, as wireworms will be sure to cause trouble under this practice.

The aeration of the soil can be increased, or even made ideal for plant roots and soil organisms, by breaking the hardpans in the subsoil. On a farm scale this can be done best by the use of a subsoiler, by planting deep-rooted cover crops or other crops, and by increasing the organic matter in the soil so that it will contain a numerous population of earthworms which will do the subsoiling. In the garden the hardpans can be broken by "trenching." This consists of digging a deep trench and throwing the soil up on the surface. Then the trench is filled by digging a second trench alongside. This is continued until the entire garden is trenched. Finally, the last trench is filled up with the soil taken out of the first trench.

Oak Smoke Method of Controlling Pests

When I was in Germany recently, I visited a drug firm whose entire output of drugs comes from plants that are grown organically: that is, without the use of chemical fertilizers or poisonous sprays, but with the use of compost. In their hothouses they have a novel way of taking care of ants, aphids, and small mites. They use the smoke from oak leaves. This practice has been long used in Germany and is a safe one, because the smoke is not a poisonous substance and will not kill bacteria in the soil, nor will it leave harmful poisonous residues on vegetables over which the smoke may be laid.

We have been using this method in our own hothouse for several years and it works very well, especially with ants. However, it should not be used when young seedlings are growing. It should be timed to take place before the crops begin to come out of the soil and when the plants have gone beyond the infant stage.

The method worked as follows: We obtained a quantity of oak leaves and placed them in a can which had a section below partitioned off by a grating. In that lower section we placed some newspaper which was set on fire. In the upper section under the leaves we placed some straw to act as a buffer between the leaves and the fire. We did not wish the former to burn, merely to smolder and to give off a thick smoke. The leaves were watered first, making sure that this was not overdone. The hothouse was closed tightly and the smoke accumulated until practically nothing could be seen within the house. It was necessary to leave it that way for about a half hour or so. We found it extremely effective in cleaning out the ants, but thoroughly! We could not find a single one after the demonstration.

Possibly there are other leaves that could be used. Books about the Hunzas of India and other tribes in that part of the world mention that many of those peoples get eye diseases because in their homes they burn birch leaves for cooking and to keep warm. I noticed statements in several such books that the birch-leaf smoke irritated the eyes of these people, causing inflammation. It may be that birch leaves are even better than oak for the purpose of insect control. This shows how an important field of research is being neglected. It is possible that some method, perhaps spraying of the soil and plants of gardens and orchards with oak smoke, using some specially developed equipment, could be very effective in keeping down the insects.

Biodynamic Sprays

The biodynamic group within the organic method has used certain kinds of sprays, in emergencies, which they claim are less harmful and which do not leave the arsenic, lead, and copper residues on the plant and soil which are so dangerous. They recommend any one of the following, but only in cases of emergency:

> Derris, containing rotenone, as spray or dust.
> Pyrethrum.
> Nicotine mixtures, such as Black Leaf 40.
> Onassia and soap solution.

They claim that these preparations disintegrate within a few days and do not permanently harm the soil. They have discovered this by experiment. However, they advise that these should not be used on any food plant within the last three weeks before it is to be eaten. The biodynamic people also use other, harmless sprays, whose effect takes a longer time to show. They contain silica, essences from manure and nasturtiums, et cetera.

Plant Neighbor Likes and Dislikes

The gardener also can control certain insects by learning the likes and dislikes of plants in relation to what grows next to them. The following notes are based on Dr. Pfeiffer's book, *Bio-Dynamic Farming and Gardening* (out of print).

BEDS. Every bed should be alternated with a bed of legumes —peas, beans, et cetera.

CARROTS. Peas are good for them when growing near by.

CELERY. Plant bush beans in next row.

CUCUMBERS. Plant beans or corn next to them. Also peas and bush beans.

FENNEL. Do not plant them near tomatoes or bush beans.

HERBS. Aromatic herbs as border plants are helpful.

KOHLRABI. Beets are good companions.

LEEKS. Do well with celery next to them.

ONIONS. Do well with beans. In poor soil, if camomile is sown thinly between, it will help.

POTATOES. Corn is a natural and beneficial neighbor. Early potatoes like beans to grow near by.

RADISHES. Will do extra well and become tender if there is a row of lettuce growing on either side of them.

SPINACH, CORN, SALAD, OR LEAF LETTUCE. Do better if grown in beds, not rows. Anything that is transplanted thrives in row formation.

TOMATOES. Plant parsley in next bed. However, do not plant next to kohlrabi. They have a harmful effect on each other.

TURNIPS. Peas are excellent neighbors.

NINETEEN

GOOD HEALTH THROUGH ORGANICALLY PRODUCED FOOD

There are two points involved here. First, will the eating of organically produced food give a person better health than the eating of food raised with chemical fertilizers? Secondly, if organic food can do this, how can the gardener have an available supply of such food? We will deal with the second part first.

The gardener should raise enough vegetables, including potatoes, not only for summer consumption but to be preserved for winter use also. He will discover that such food not only tastes better but has additional health and taste advantages because of its freshness, because it gets to the table quicker. If he lives on the outskirts of a town or in the country, he could raise rabbits or chickens, attempting to grow some of their food organically. This will also give him his own supply of manure, making him feel that he is part of a cycle. Perhaps he can have a goat. And if he is not sensitive to poison ivy, he can pick wild food in the hedgerows along the countryside—dandelion, wild strawberries, herbs, and a host of other nutritious items. Perhaps a friendly farmer will sell him some alfalfa cut right from the growing plants in the field. Alfalfa can be eaten if chopped into mashed potatoes or steeped into tea, et cetera.

Many busy people who have no time can afford to pay a high-school boy to work part time at making a vegetable garden. Then, of course, there are sources where many kinds of organically produced foods may be purchased. Consult the columns of *Organic Gardening* for names. One should also use salt-water fish for a prominent portion of the diet. Here is a wonderful, mineral-laden food, including iodine, which does not harbor the effects of chemical fertilizers. Cows may be fed on commercial, devitalized grains, but the fish in the sea still feed the way they always have. I cannot stress this point too much. Eat a lot of salt-water fish (not fresh-water types, which may be polluted), grow your own vegetables, and you are on the road to health improvement which will amaze you.

Now, coming back to the first part of our two-part question, will the eating of organically produced food make a person healthier? There is so much medical evidence that it will that it isn't even funny. It is incredibly tragic that those who are in charge of the public's nutrition do not use their weight to make such food available to the public. Hundreds of physicians have gone on record testifying to its health-giving qualities. Thousands of doctors are applying it in their own gardens and farms, yet they are doing little to spread the idea.

The September 1953 issue of the *International Record of Medicine and General Practice Clinics* contains an article written by W. Coda Martin, M.D., of New York City. When an orthodox medical journal publishes an article which endorses the organic method it *is* an event. But it is the beginning of a trend. Once the ice is broken there will be a general and regular increase in the medical acceptance of our method.

Dr. Martin states that a large portion of the degenerative diseases today are the result of prolonged malnutrition; that we are starving in the midst of plenty; that the U. S. Plant, Soil and Nutrition Laboratory at Cornell has stated that some of the main fruit- and vegetable-growing soils in the eastern seaboard are so mineral-deficient that they lack the protective qualities which such foods are supposed to give; that the average person's diet does not contain adequate amounts of calcium; that such deficient diets will ultimately lead to degenerative disease; that foods grown on fertile soils will prevent such disease; that scientists formerly believed longevity to be due to heredity but were changing over to give nutrition an important place in the prolongation of life.

The article gives much valuable information on how and what to eat in order to become healthier, but the amazing thing is that, in concluding, Dr. Martin says: "Organically grown foods are advisable when available for consumption," specifically stating that organic foods are 20 to 40 per cent richer in vitamins and trace minerals, while being free from the poison-spray residues which sometimes produce liver damage in humans. "For optimum health," the doctor concludes, "this type of food is essential."

After this was written I found another tribute to the organic method, which appeared in the September 30, 1953, issue of the *Medical Press,* a medical journal published in London, England. It deals with a new book by Lady Louise Howard, entitled *Sir Albert Howard in India.* The review follows:

"The late Sir Albert Howard will, we believe, in years to come, be regarded as one of the outstanding spirits of our age. His subject, unfortunately for his reputation, is not one to attract headlines in the daily Press at the moment, though as the years go on we believe his teachings will be found of increasing importance to the welfare, not only of the inhabitants of these islands and of India, but of the whole human race. Sir Albert, we should remember, began his career as an agricultural chemist and research worker, first of all in the West Indies and later in India where the great bulk of his life's work was done. The final chapter in his career, which was almost entirely devoted to making propaganda for his views, eventually thrust him into considerable prominence in this country, though to most of those who were unaware of his previous work his stature did not achieve the dimensions which it is bound ultimately to attain.

"This book, by his second wife, gives a most interesting and largely factual account of his work in India. His first task was the examination of methods of wheat growing in the sub-continent and ended in the development of superior strains of wheat, which alone have contributed enormously to India's well-being. This was followed by penetrating studies of irrigation, soil drainage and aeration, and the causes of soil erosion, and led finally to his grappling boldly with the problem of disease. It was this last above all which led him to the annunciation of his own organic doctrines. What this book will do above all is to show him for what he was, a many-sided man of genius who never left a problem until he had solved it, equally original in his approach to ecology whether in the plains or on the hills, or in his dealing with the peasants or his Indian colleagues. Above all he was a scientist of enough intellectual power and imagination to see clearly and acutely the defects of the too narrow scientific approach. Many of his critics in later years seemed to regard him as an ignorant fanatic, though as we have seen he was trained as a scientist, achieved eminence as such, and practiced scientific methods with notable success. He only reluctantly parted company with orthodox science when he found its theories and practice unyielding in face of the facts.

If at the close of his career he tended to express himself with more vehemence than charity, this was merely reaction to the opposition which his doctrines aroused, and (as it seemed to him) unaccountably aroused since they were based on the most painstaking observation and practice. His day will surely come, and that before long."

If this were the kind of book that required it, I could produce irrefutable evidence from many other scientific sources to prove that human health can be improved, and disease reduced, by the eating of organically produced food, but *Organic Gardening* is not that kind of book. Suffice it to say that we have many letters from readers of our magazines to the effect that they and their families have noticed improvements in their health. We have proved it in an experiment with mice that were divided into two groups. The record in my own case is quite dramatic. I tried many systems that failed until I came upon this bonanza.

If you have never gardened organically, what wonderful pleasures await you! What untold delights can be yours! It is a new world that you can enter. I am reminded of an experience several years ago when I gave a talk to the botany class at Wellesley College. I was told in advance that a ninety-three-year-old gentleman would be sitting in the front row and would come up to speak to me after my talk. This he did, and it was a most pleasant experience. The head of the botany department told me that about two years before, the old man's wife had died and it had made him lose all interest in life, a thing which often happens to very old people who have had a long and happy life together. When one goes the other soon follows, because there is no will to live. His friends were greatly concerned about him and searched frantically for ways to stir up the old man's interest in living. Finally one of them succeeded.

He suggested that the old man become interested in organic gardening, for the gardening urge was very strong in him. All his life he had had a garden.

They described all the advantages of the organic method, and as they spoke a glow seemed to come into the old man's eyes. He looked backward upon an entire lifetime, since boyhood—eighty years—and began to wonder. Had he been gardening in a dark alley all those years? He recalled continuous warfare with the insect and the whole array of poisonous insecticides that were on his shelves, besides the sacks of chemicals. Yet, hazily, his mind brought up vague remembrances of pleasant gardening experiences in his more youthful years, when the chemicalization of garden and farm had not yet blossomed forth in its vicious powerfulness as in the last fifteen years or so. He recalled the fruit orchards of his early youth which yielded eatable apples without the use of poisonous insecticides.

He was given a gift subscription to *Organic Gardening* and purchased a few booklets to get enough information to begin the new method the next spring. All through the winter he planned and dreamed. He had secured a new lease on life.

In the spring his gardener began making compost and the old man watched over it every day as if it were a precious child. That same year they began to spread the compost, and exactly as the literature said, it all became re-created under his eyes. Never in all his rememberable years had he had such an abundance and lushness of vegetables, with so little of disease and insect infestation. He had more happiness in those summer days of only one season than during the last fifty years. His body seemed to become stronger; his will to live soared.

He came over to speak to me when my talk to the botany class of Wellesley was concluded and thanked me for having published the information which had opened his eyes. You can imagine my feelings.

It is in this spirit that I wish to close this book. There are infinite pleasures awaiting you if you have never gardened organically.

INDEX

Russell, quoted, 87–88
Rusts, 188–89

"Salt sickness" disease, 164
Sanitation, 187, 195, 200, 202
Sassafras oil, 197
Sawdust, 84, 93, 163
Scales, 201
Scarseth, George D., quoted, 74–75
Seaweed, 70, 130
Seed germination, 65
Selvi, Charles, 112, 114–15
Sheet composting, 80–81
Silos, carbon dioxide in, 39
Slag, 172–73
Slate residues, 172–73
Slugs, 192, 201–2
Smoke, oak leaf, 203–5
Snow, benefits from, 156–57
Soap solution, 205
Sod, wireworms in, 203
Sodas, 23, 143
Sodium carbonate, 39
Soil, 11–12, 19–33, 78–80, 143, 191
  acid, 14, 202–3
  aeration of, 24, 40, 51, 80–81, 114, 136, 203
  alkaline, 163, 186
  antibiotic aspects of, 48–50
  ants in, 195
  biology of, 23, 47–48
  chemistry of, 20–23, 40–43, 45, 85–86, 141
  color of, 61–65, 117
  definition of, 19
  desert, 31
  fertility of, 64–65, 67–68, 103, 112, 163, 187
  importance of nitrogen to,

67–81
  infertile, use of, 13
  mineralizing of, 31–33
  plant disease and, 187–88, 190
  poison sprays and, 179–80
  rocks and, 158–59, 164–65, 170, 173
  and soil conditioners, 133–39, 151
  temperature and, 65
  volcanic, 64
Soil conditioners, 133–39, 151
Soil erosion, 44, 137, 158
Soil and Health Foundation, 112
Soil-till, 172
Sowbugs, 202
Soybeans, 87, 197
Spiders, 194, 200
Spraying, 12, 175–81
Sprays, biodynamic, 205
  harmless, 195, 198, 201, 205
  poison, 16, 50, 53–55, 139, 143–44, 175, 200, 209
Squash bugs, 202
Stark Bros. Nurseries, 120
Stilbestrol, 139
Stone meal, 166
Streptomycin, 49
Subsoil, 24–27, 30–33, 203
Sulphates, 143
Sulphur, 23, 44, 60–61, 73, 157, 162, 186
Sunlight, 40
Superphosphates, 23, 52–53, 161–62
Swanson, C. L., 136–37
Sweet clover, 88–89, 201
Switzerland, soil of, 158
Systox, 177–78